CHEVROLET CORVETTE

1953-86

CHEVROLET CORVETTE

1953-86

A Documentation by Walter Zeichner

1469 Morstein Road, West Chester, Pennsylvania 19380

General Motors lauded this racy two-seater as the only true sports car of America when they introduced it in 1953. In fact, this car ranked among the most fascinating that Detroit had ever offered. An overview of the wealth of advertising materials and press reports of thirty years, chosen with love and reprinted in this book, makes clear why the Corvette was so successful. For this car was anything but the typical "Detroit Bathtub"—the Corvette was always a car with its own character.

The documents were gathered by Walter Zeichner with the assistance of Kai Jacobsen, to whom we express our particular thanks.

Halwart Schrader
Editor

Translated from the German by Dr. Edward Force.

Copyright © 1989 by Schiffer Publishing Ltd.
Library of Congress Catalog Number: 89-084169.

Printed in the United States of America.
ISBN: 0-88740-194-5
Published by Schiffer Publishing Ltd.
1469 Morstein Road, West Chester, Pennsylvania 19380

Originally published under the title "Chevrolet Corvette" 1953-86, Schrader Motor Chronik, copyright Schrader Automobil-Bücher, Handels-GmbH, München, West Germany, © 1986, ISBN: 3-922617-51-4.

Contents

Page

A Sports Car Made in U.S.A.

The Corvette was, and still is today, the only genuine sports car in production in America, if one disregards a few short-lived "one-day flights". This fact is all the more astounding when one considers the high position that motor sports have long held in the USA.

There was always a very high demand for sports cars, of course, but it was met almost exclusively by products made in Europe.

The story of the Chevrolet Corvette's origin is closely linked with the designer Harley Earl, who had had the idea of a reasonably priced, simply built sports car as early as 1951, and who finally was able to make it happen and build such a car.

Earl had come to General Motors in 1932, after studying at Stanford and spending some time designing special bodies for an extravagant clientele in Hollywood. At GM he had established a Design Center that at that time had no equal, and in which people worked who had a decisive effect on the style of the American car: standards were set by the "Dream Cars" displayed at shows and Motoramas, cars with strikingly futuristic styling and extravagant details that afforded a look into the future of the automobile, at least in the USA, and which drew crowds of car fans. Such creations were a specialty of Harley Earl. With his "Buick Y-Job", displayed in 1938, he influenced the ideal of American car styling into the late Forties.

After World War II, during which the American automotive giants had been busy with the production of war materials and the manufacture of civilian cars had rested, production was at first recommenced with the old models, before new elements of style became visible from all American automobile manufacturers by the beginning of the Fifties.

One of these trend-setters was the Buick "Le Sabre", which Earl designed, a prototype influenced by jet plane styling, that caused a sensation at shows in 1951, and some of the outstanding characteristics of which, like the extremely panoramic windshields and the folding top disappearing under a cover, were to be inherited by the later Corvette.

In the same year, Harley Earl and a small staff of personal colleagues, working in a separate studio, began to develop a sports car. At first it was planned to build a two-seater in the price range of ordinary Chevrolet or Ford sedans. The first drawings showed a car that looked like a cross between a Jaguar XK 120 and a Jeepster, based on a normal production sedan chassis. The work was done under the name "Project Opel", for much stress was put on strict secrecy, even inside the factory, which had often taken on design work for GM's German descendant.

In 1952 Edward Cole joined the team, a builder who was to determine the technical aspect of the future Corvette. Soon both departments worked together closely. Earl's team got ever farther from the modest initial plans and now oriented themselves stylistically to the Dream Cars like the Buick Le Sabre and the new XP-300, an even more futuristic model.

Meanwhile it was decided that the car was to be built with the slightest possible need for parts that had to be made new, for in the directors' offices an expensive "toy", of which only a few would sell, would have fallen on deaf ears. So construction had to proceed on the principle that as many parts as

How happy the general manager's wife is—the caption of this press photo of 1960 could read something like that. Knock-off hubcaps and whitewall tires were always popular.

possible could be taken "from the stock" of contemporary production parts, which included as good as all mechanical parts and the chassis. The body was also to be as cheap to build as possible.

Now the Chevrolet Division had already tested a large convertible with a reinforced fiberglass body. The new material had even survived an unintentional accident by the test driver almost undamaged. This was just what Harley Earl wanted, for this easily formed new material would save the enormous costs of body tooling, which meant that his "baby" would add up to an even lower investment risk for the firm. The chances of clearance for series production increased; how the plastic material would perform in years of everyday use was another question.

Meanwhile it had become the summer of 1952, and

The 1964 Sting Ray coupe. Was flying nicer? The air captain and the stewardess had voted in favor of the Corvette . . .

a finished clay model of the new two-seater stood in the development department of the Art & Color Studios. Chevrolet Chief Engineer Ed Cole was also excited about the car. Now came the great moment—the showing of the model to General Motors President Harlow Curtice and the top Chevrolet officials. The new sports car pleased the august gentlemen so much that a prototype was ordered, in order to display it to the public at the first Motorama. Such a car, they were sure, would particularly improve the image of the whole Chevrolet line.

The construction of the prototype now proceeded at top speed, and now it had to be fully functioning under the hood too. Suspension specialist Maurice Olley found a way to build a suitable chassis and suspension of mainly production parts that could

easily be modified to meet the demands of a sports car. This had a positive effect on the costs, even though the car could not compete with European products in terms of construction.

On January 17, 1953 the veil was finally lifted. In the grand ballroom of the Waldorf-Astoria Hotel in New York, visitors to the first Motorama of the year crowded around the white roadster made by Chevrolet. The wheelbase of the two-seater, named "Corvette" by Chevrolet, was exactly that of the Jaguar XK 120, but the car was wider and heavier. Styling borrowed from European sports-car manufacturing was clearly avoided. For optimal weight distribution, the seats were placed just in front of the rear axle. The motor, a souped-up "Blue Flame" straight-six producing 150 HP, could be installed quite far back, dividing the weight 53 to 47 between the front and rear axles. A radiator grille with big chrome teeth dominated the front, which was protected only by bumper overriders left and right of the license plate and on the corners; sporty stone grids decorated the oval headlights set deep in the rounded front fenders.

A low panoramic windshield bordered the interior, which was finished in red imitation leather; the chrome windshield frame was continued in a ring surrounding the entire cockpit. The dashboard was also very reminiscent of the Dream Cars. The speedometer was on the left, the radio loudspeaker and glove compartment on the right. Between them, no fewer than six instruments looked at the passengers, the largest of them, in the middle, being the tachometer. The bucket seats were bedded in the chassis, and the doors of the prototype opened at the push of a button. The light top with snap-on windows disappeared under a cover behind the seats. The tail was rounded like the nose, but here definite tailfins were modeled, with round taillights at the top and small torpedo wings. The big wheel wells gave a clear view of the whitewall tires, and a lateral chrome strip running from the front bumpers to the rear ones flanked the big side panels.

Without a doubt, it was a very well-designed and pleasing car that the people in New York could admire. Almost four million examined the new model. The reactions were overwhelming. Harley Earl had made his dream come true—the firm's management gave the order to put the Corvette into production as fast as possible.

The first 300 pre-production Corvettes were produced, chiefly by hand, before the end of 1953, while a new production line was set up in St. Louis, where the Corvette was manufactured until 1981. At that time the 46 fiberglass body parts were produced by a separate firm in Ohio and then glued together by hand, while the motors came from the Chevrolet motor plant in New York. A subcontractor also assembled the chassis. These first cars were not yet perfect in terms of workmanship, and the first 25 also had Chevrolet "Bel Air" sedan production hubcaps, used before the Corvette's own knock-off hubcaps existed (which many regarded as hardly in good taste). All 300 cars were sprayed in "Polo White" and had red and white interiors with black tops and whitewall tires.

Unfortunately, the car's performance disappointed the first testers and owners, as it was in no way able to fulfill their high expectations. The six-cylinder motor barely let the car, which for reasons of cost and space had been fitted with the well-known "Power-glide" two-speed automatic transmission, reach 170 kph. And an acceleration time of at best 11 seconds for zero to 100 kph was not likely to excite the spoiled American public either. At the same time, the intended low price had not been realizable by a long way, and so the roadster cost a hefty $3513.

For the 1954 model year, production in St. Louis turned out approximately 50 cars a day. During the course of the year, the Corvette was improved in several ways. The sports car could be had in metallic blue as well as polo white, but only 4% chose the third possibility, "Sportsman Red". In addition, of the 3640 Corvettes produced in that year, just six had a special black paint job with red interior.

To open the doors of the production Corvette there was no longer a push-button as in the prototype; rather one had to reach through the window—which was no fun at all with the top up—and pull the inside lever backward. But the position of the choke, which in the first cars was still at right next to the ignition lock, meaning that one had to reach through the steering wheel with one's left hand while turning the ignition key with the right, was improved. The tops of the 1954 models were brown.

The body also caused problems, since it allowed water leaks in several places, a problem that could only be eliminated during the course of the model year. And the public's lack of interest in the Corvette was something to worry about: the critics had obviously judged the car too harshly. Accustomed by now to European styling and high-performance motors, the public found scarcely anything good in the Chevrolet. In many opinions, the car lacked the quickness of a sports car. The automatic transmission and ordinary motor, along with the chunky body, could not compete with a Jaguar, and on the other hand, the car was too uncomfortable for a tourer. At the end of 1954, almost 1500 cars still stood on dealers' lots. But there was good news for the 1955 model year, for the new V8 motor created by Ed Cole, producing 195 HP and yet 15 kg lighter than the old six-cylinder, was available optionally. This first V8 Corvette reached 100 kph in just 8.5 seconds—so nobody could complain about lacking power any more.

The automatic transmission did not fit the image of a sports car either, but it remained in production for the time being. In this model year the car attracted only 700 buyers, of whom all of ten chose the old six-cylinder type. Whoever wanted a "real" sports car had, after all, a large selection of chic cars from Europe to choose from, and whoever wanted American comfort but with sporting atmosphere and high performance, bought the new Ford Thunderbird, which perfectly combined sedanlike comfort with pseudo-sporting qualities and sold more than 20 times as well as the Corvette, whose days seemed to be numbered.

But General Motors certainly did not want to lose the race against the Ford Motor Company under any conditions. Finally a man appeared who was to guide the destiny of this American sports car for many years: Zora Arkus-Duntov. Born in Belgium and formerly a builder for the British sports-car firm of Allard, he had come to GM in the year of the Corvette's birth and soon took charge of the unsuccessful sports car. The new 1956 model was to be decisively influenced by him. Above all, the body was completely reworked, with considerable changes made to the front half. A wide channel was cast into the sides, running from the wheel wells to just under the new door handles and spray-painted a contrasting color. The headlights were now vertical and had no protective grid any more. The fins disappeared from the tail, and nicely curved fenders remained, with the two exhaust pipes coming out their ends; on previous models they had emerged near the trunk lid and, thanks to swirling exhaust gas, always got the roadster's tail dirty. For the comfort-conscious American sports-car driver, the car now had cranked windows, and an optional hardtop made the Corvette into a coupe.

The car could now be ordered in seven colors, with more or less tasteful interior contrasts. But the changes in the second-generation Corvette were in no way limited to external things. The active racing driver Arkus-Duntov had given a lot of attention to the handling characteristics (only the brakes were, alas, still very inadequate, and quickly reacted to sporting driving by fading). But most of all, the Corvette now had a three-speed gearbox instead of the automatic transmission, along with a motor whose performance had been increased again. The most powerful sedan motor with quadruple carburetion had been tuned, through the addition of a camshaft "sharpened" by Duntov, to give 225 HP at 5200 rpm; with the manual transmission, the new Corvette stormed to 100 kph in a respectable 7.5 seconds, and this even with the long ratio of 3.27 : 1.

In 1958 there was another significant face-lifting, with double headlights, additional front air intakes and a lot more chrome; all in all, the car was almost 100 kilos heavier but hardly better looking; it now seemed quite overloaded. Inside there was a completely new dashboard in the form of two semicircular insets. The right one had a heavy handhold in front of it, to which the passenger could cling during bold maneuvers, and on the driver's side all the instruments except the clock had been gathered, crowned by a huge semicircular speedometer.

For motive power there was still only the 283-cubic-inch powerplant with output between 230 (with quadruple carburetor) and 315 HP (with fuel injection) available until 1961. No Corvette now took longer than 8 seconds to reach 100 kph.

In 1961—now under the direction of new chief designer Bill Mitchell, who had created the futuristic "Stingray" and "XP-700" dream cars—the round rear end was replaced by a "ducktail". The trend moved toward more angular forms. In the following year the side panels became simpler, and there was also a bigger V8 motor again, now with 327 cubic inches. With carburetors these motors produced between 250 and 340 HP, and a version with the enormously high compression ratio of 11.25 : 1 and fuel injection produced as much as 360 HP. By now such a car cost just over $5000.

Much resembling the "Stingray" prototype in styling, the fourth-generation Corvette appeared in 1963 in roadster and hardtop form, as well as a new coupe with unusual styling, its fastback running to a point, with double rear windows and doors reaching well into the roof—one of the most sought-after Corvette variations today. Bill Mitchell had developed the new style, with its shark nose and mouth and, compared to earlier models, more angular lines. But a lot had happened under the plastic hood too. A new ladder frame made it possible to mount the seats even deeper and farther back, for optimal weight distribution. The wheelbase had been shortened, and the rear wheels had finally been suspended independently, which much improved the car's roadholding.

For the 1963 model year the previous year's motors had been retained, but from 1964 on, and till the end of this body type in 1967, another big increase in performance had taken place. In 1964 there were six performance types of the 327-cubic-inch motor, from 250 to 375 HP, but that was only a tame beginning.

In 1965—the same year that brought optional four-wheel disc brakes for the first time—there came a new 396-cubic-inch carbureted motor producing 425 HP, along with a sporty suspension and visible signs like a big power bulge on the motor hood and side exhaust pipes, all of which turned the Chevy sports car into an exciting vehicle.

From that year on, there were no more fuel injected motors, on account of costs, but by now the Corvette had developed into a sales success. Almost 120,000 of this body type alone were sold, of which more than 72,000 were roadsters.

Work on a successor model had begun as early as 1963/64. It was to be a beautiful mid-engined experimental car with the designation "XP-882", which was canceled soon afterward for reasons of cost. The new Corvette was built quite conventionally. Its model was the almost evil-looking "Mako Shark II" styling study of 1965, which was made into a somewhat moderated but still very aggressive-looking sports car under the direction of the new art director, David Holls.

The critics had always had much to criticize in what was probably the Corvette style best known in Europe. It was too big, too old-fashioned, and there was too little room inside for passengers and luggage. Despite all that, 28,566 buyers were not put off from buying it in the 1968 model year—a new record. This body style was built until 1983, with numerous changes. There were three varieties until the roadster was dropped in 1976, a new "T-top" convertible with removable roof panels and a coupe.

Strict exhaust laws reduced the performance of the strongest version to 365 HP in 1972, and after a few intermediate stops, and because of the petroleum shortage, it reached 205 HP in 1975. The Corvette had changed from a strong-as-a-bear "muscle car" to a car equipped with all imaginable extras and meant for sport-minded housewives, even though it had room for only two full supermarket grocery bags. It was no wonder that fewer and fewer buyers were interested in the sports car that was overweight and weak in comparison to earlier versions. So the sales figures for 1975—the last year of the Sting Ray roadster—sank to a meager 4629 cars.

Fully ten years were to pass before a really new Corvette would see the light of day, developed by a new team of constructors and designers—unburdened by the past. The strikingly low and wide coupe that introduced the sixth generation of this sports car in 1983 was again inspired by numerous show cars, and one must admit that it has become a very impressive car. It makes the traditional characteristics of the Corvette, symbolized power and pouncing quickness, come to life again. Intensive developmental work on this wedge-shaped car, which took form under the clear influence of the wind tunnel, had begun in 1978. Except for its width, it is smaller in every dimension than the Sting Ray, but looks much prettier thanks to clever revision of its proportions. The high point of the new 230 HP Corvette was reached in 1986 with the introduction of a roadster version, the first in ten years. This was a modern, capably designed vehicle—worthy of continuing the series of impressive open sports cars from Chevrolet since 1953.

With its inherited 6-cylinder Chevy motor—even producing 150 HP—the Corvette was not a very hot number. And despite the great interest that the car had awakened when introduced, only 4000 customers bought this car in 1953-54. But the production possibilities were limited at first also.

The Chevrolet Corvette . . .

outstanding performance . . .

amazing acceleration . . . very low center of gravity

WINDSHIELD — Chrome-bound, one-piece, curved Safety Plate Glass; 55-degree slant.. HOOD—Glass-fiber hood, with hinges at front. HEADLIGHTS—Recessed in fenders; parking lights beside ends of radiator grille. RADIATOR GRILLE—Chrome airscoop radiator grille. FRONT GUARDS—Chrome grille guard; chrome fender guards. FRONT SUSPENSION—Knee Action, with direct double-acting shock absorbers, and ride stabilizer. STEERING—Full anti-friction steering gear, Center-Point Steering linkage.

Little information is given in the first brochure that was given out by General Motors when production began in the summer of 1953. The many chromed parts are noted with pride.

HEIGHT—33″ at door; 47″ at windshield. LENGTH—102″ wheelbase; 167″ over-all. WIDTH—70″ over-all. WEIGHT—Approximately 2900 pounds curb weight. TOP—Rakish, manually adjusted, lightweight fabric top; folds into concealed compartment at front of rear deck. BODY—Special open-cockpit, 2-passenger, glass-fiber body. ENGINE—160-h.p. high-compression 6-cylinder valve-in-head special "Blue Flame" Engine, with triple side-draft carburetors and dual exhaust system. TRANSMISSION—Powerglide Automatic Transmission, with floor-mounted selector lever. WHEELS—6.70 x 15, whitewall tires; chrome wheel disks with simulated "knock-off" hubs. Front tread, 57″; rear tread, 59″. BRAKES—Hydraulic 4-wheel 11″ Jumbo-Drum self-energizing brakes, with bonded linings. Mechanical actuation of rear wheel brakes for parking. CHASSIS FRAME—X-member-braced Box Girder Frame. GASOLINE TANK—18 gallons behind seats; concealed filler on left side.

13

Real driving comfort . . . the Corvette way!

SECURITY AND LUXURY for driver and passenger are the keynotes of the snug Corvette cockpit. Individual bucket seats have form-fitting foam rubber cushions. The floor is covered in soft carpeting, backed by sponge rubber. Large pockets and ash trays in doors also serve as arm rests. Beautifully balanced instrument panel includes key-turn starter, electric clock, tachometer, hooded radio speaker.

POTENT "BLUE-FLAME" 6 engine, with three side-draft carburetors, 8 to 1 compression ratio, and overhead valves, puts a flashing 155 horsepower under the throttle. It has a dual exhaust system, efficient cooling and lubrication, and a shielded electrical system . . . plus Chevrolet's traditional six-cylinder economy of operation and maintenance.

14

In the 1954 model year there were Corvettes with a V8 motor too; a year later the car gained cranked door windows and—optionally—a hardtop. The car began to interest the Americans.

Left and right: A small folding card of 1955, in two colors and without exaggerations. Stone guards in front of the headlights were regarded as particularly sporting.

SPECIFICATIONS

POWER-PACKED CHASSIS

ENGINES—Choice of 195-h.p. "Turbo-Fire V8" with 4-barrel carburetor; or 155-h.p. "Blue-Flame" Six with 3 side-draft carburetors. Valve-in-head design, 8:1 compression ratio, high-lift camshaft, dual exhaust system, shielded ignition.

TRANSMISSION—Powerglide Automatic Transmission. Floor-mounted selector lever.

DRIVE LINE—Hotchkiss drive. Hypoid axle; 3.55:1 with Powerglide Automatic Transmission.

TIRES—Five 6.70-15 tubeless tires.

STEERING—Anti-friction gear, 16 to 1 ratio; balanced linkage. Nearly vertical, 17¼ two-spoke steering wheel.

BRAKES—Hydraulic, 11" self-energizing brakes; bonded linings. Pull-handle parking brake.

SUSPENSION—Independent front suspension, ride stabilizer. Four-leaf rear springs, outrigger mounted. Direct double-acting shock absorbers.

FRAME—Extra-rigid X-member-braced box girder frame.

FUEL TANK—Capacity: 17 gal. Concealed side filler.

LIGHTWEIGHT BODY

BODY—2-passenger, open-cockpit body of glass-fiber-reinforced plastic; light, strong, durable, quiet, rustproof, and easy to repair. Wide doors with inside release.

COMPARTMENTS—Front-hinged hood with automatically latching support. Large luggage locker with spare-wheel well under floor, and lockable counterbalanced lid. Concealed well for top in rear deck behind seats. Saddle-covered door pockets.

WINDOWS AND TOP—Chrome-bound, one-piece, curved safety plate glass windshield; 53-degree slant. Removable chrome-bound plastic side windows with ventipanes. Manually adjusted fabric top with plastic rear window.

COLORS—Exterior: Polo White or Pennant Blue. Cockpit: Sportsman Red or Beige seat and side wall upholstery; red- or blue-crowned white instrument panel; red or beige carpet. Luggage Locker: Sportsman Red or Beige. Top: Tan.

CAR DIMENSIONS—Wheelbase, 102". Length, 167". Height, 33" at door top. Road Clearance, 6". Width, 70". Tread, 57" front, 59" rear.

All illustrations and specifications contained in this literature are based on the latest product information available at the time of approval. The right is reserved to make changes at any time without notice in price, color, materials, equipment, specifications, and model, and also to discontinue model.

CHEVROLET MOTOR DIVISION, GENERAL MOTORS CORPORATION, DETROIT 2, MICHIGAN

LITHO IN U.S.A.

New 195-h.p. Chevrolet Corvette

V8

A brilliant new edition of America's most popular production sports car

A touch and she's up!

The new power-operated fabric top (now available in white with black and beige, optionally keyed to exterior color) folds out of sight under its covered compartment. Wider windows increase visibility.

Quick change! A roadster or coupe!

A smartly-conceived plastic hardtop featuring a wrap-around rear window is available at extra cost. It is easily and securely installed with only five knurled set screws.

Let it rain, let it snow

Corvette offers the convenience of new "roll-up" regulators to quickly raise and lower the new side windows. Power window lifts, only one of Corvette's several new power features, are available at extra cost.

New "going" look

Now Corvette is even more adventurous-looking with graceful new fenderlines, new side panel and hood treatment and simulated knock-off type wheel covers.

New "out-front" styling

The raised forward portion of the fender houses an improved design headlight that projects forward to extend the fenderline and contributes to Corvette's rakish look.

Eight-Jet take-offs!

The Corvette's 265-cubic-inch V8 engine owes its greater horsepower to dual 4-barrel carburetion, higher compression ratio and new manifolds with "twin pipe" exhausts.

This folding card was similar to that on pages 14/15. But: the stone guards have disappeared, and a curved bar decorates the flanks. The '56 Corvette has become attractive . . .

NEW

Corvette

Since its initial introduction in limited volume Corvette has commanded the attention of sport enthusiasts. Now its major new design factors w welcomed as answers to the needs expressed by well-informed group. Drivers who scorn the "s

16

SPECIFICATIONS

ENGINE

"Turbo-Fire Special V8." Valve-in-head design, 265-cubic-inch displacement, 3.75" bore x 3.0" stroke, 9.25:1 compression ratio. 225 horsepower at 5200 rpm. Torque 270 foot-pounds at 3600 rpm. Special high-lift camshaft, high-speed valve mechanism. Polished aluminum rocker covers. Dual four-barrel carburetion, buff aluminum racing-type air cleaners, special intake manifold. Full pressure lubrication system with full-flow oil filter.* High-power exhaust headers and full dual exhaust system. Shielded ignition, 12-volt electrical system. Engine precision balanced after assembly.

TRANSMISSION

Choice of special high-performance 3-speed close-ratio Synchro-Mesh (2.2:1 low and reverse, 1.31:1 second, 1.1 high) with high-capacity 10-inch coil-spring clutch, or optional Powerglide special automatic transmission.* Floor mounted gear or range selector.

REAR AXLE

High torque capacity axle; 3.55:1 ratio standard, 3.27:1 ratio optional with either Synchro-Mesh or Powerglide.

CHASSIS

Extra-rigid X-member-braced box girder frame. Independent coil front suspension with ride stabilizer. Self-lubricating four-leaf rear springs, outrigger mounted. Direct double-acting shock absorbers. Full anti-friction 16:1 ratio steering gear, balanced linkage. Competition-type steering wheel with three shock absorbing spring-steel spokes. Hydraulic 11-inch self-energizing brakes with new bonded linings, pull-handle parking brake. Suspended brake pedal. Choice of black or white sidewall* standard 6.70-15-4 ply tubeless tires or optional 6.70-15-4 ply high-speed nylon racing type.* Decorative wheel covers with simulated knock-off knobs. 17-gallon fuel tank with concealed side filler.

BODY FEATURES

Glass-fiber-reinforced plastic with sculptured side panels; light, strong, durable, quiet, rustproof, easy to repair. Distinctive embossed hood, front hinged, with automatic support, inside release. Simulated twin fender air scoops. Two-passenger compartment, large luggage locker with spare-wheel well under floor, concealed top well behind seats. Unique Corvette crossed-flag emblems on hood and trunk lid. Twin exhaust ports integral with rear bumpers. Chrome-bound, one-piece, curved safety plate glass windshield. Power-operated fabric top with wide plastic rear window. Richly trimmed quick-change hardtop* with rear-quarter windows and full-vision rear window.

INTERIOR FEATURES

Form-fitting vinyl-covered seats, individually adjustable, with safety belt.* Wide doors with built-in arm rest, push-button door handle, key lock, inside door release, swing-out door hinges. Choice of crank-operated or power* window lifts. Ash tray and glove compartment between seats; padded roll on instrument panel and doors, rubber-backed carpeting, metal door kick panels, sills, and step plates. Signal-seeking radio,* heater,* directional signals, electric clock, cigarette lighter, tachometer, outside and inside rear-view mirror, windshield washer.*

COLORS

Onyx Black with Red interior and Black or White top, Venetian Red with Red interior and Beige or White top, Cascade Green with Beige interior and Beige or White top, Aztec copper with Beige interior and Beige or White top, Arctic Blue with Beige or Red interior and Beige or White top, Polo White with Red interior and White or Black top.

DIMENSIONS

Wheelbase, 102". Length, 168.01". Overall height: top down, 49.20"; Convertible top, 51.09"; hardtop, 50.98". Height at door 32.55". Road clearance 6". Width, 70.46". Tread, 57" front, 59" rear.

*Optional at extra cost.

All illustrations and specifications contained in this literature are based on the latest information available at the time of publication approval. The right is reserved to make changes at any time without notice in price, color, materials, equipment and specifications.

CHEVROLET MOTOR DIVISION • GENERAL MOTORS CORPORATION • DETROIT 2, MICHIGAN

LITHO IN U.S.A.

The technical data of the 1956 model. The choice of body colors is noteworthy!

own convertible" and will accept nothing less than an authentic, competition-type sports car will quickly sense that *action* is the keynote of the new Corvette V8. But convenience is accented too, and you will find many luxury features seldom available in a car of this caliber.

Live, Lithe, Luxurious Action

A brochure from the summer of 1956, now printed in four colors and with a lot of interesting detail photos. Much was new in the Corvette—see below.

Close-up details reveal *New* Corvette Advancements

A touch . . . and she's up!

The new power-operated fabric top (now available in white with black and beige keyed to exterior color) folds out of sight under its plastic-lidded compartment behind the seat. Wider rear window and new-design side windows increase visibility.

This . . . is for the "Box Boys"

The new Corvette with a new floor-mounted "stick" shift close ratio Synchro-Mesh transmission. Here is the split-second up-shifting, down-shifting, close-ratio gear control demanded by the experts!

Eight-Jet Carburetion for take-offs!

The Corvette's 265-cubic-inch V8 engine owes its greater horsepower to dual 4-barrel carburetion, higher compression ratio and new manifolds with "twin pipe" exhausts.

Avant-Garde styling with a touch of tradition

The Corvette is a true sports car—not a scaled-down convertible. Now it's even more adventurous-looking with graceful new fender lines, new side panel and hood treatment and simulated knock-off type wheel covers.

Quick change! A roadster or coupe!

A plastic hardtop featuring a wraparound rear window is available as extra cost equipment. It is easily and securely installed with only five knurled set screws.

Let it rain, let it snow!

Corvette offers the convenience of roll-up regulators that quickly raise and lower the new windows. Power window lifts are available as an extra cost option.

A hood full of "Horses" add a carload of Safety!

The new "Turbo-fire V8" engine is a real life-saver when only sheer *passing power* can leave hazards behind and whisk you to safety. New cylinder heads up Corvette's compression ratio to 9.25 to 1!

"Out-front" styling for looking ahead

The raised-forward portion of the fender houses an improved design headlight that projects forward to extend the fender-line and contribute to Corvette's rakish look.

18

A NEW CORVETTE
BY CHEVROLET

Now even greater than the original in . . .

Looks and Performance!

The title page of this brochure expresses speed, yet one finds no reference to top speed. It was sufficient to speak of "high speed racing tires" and plentiful horse-power...

Sensational to GO in . . .

So smart to be SEEN in . . .

So comfortable to BE in!

The new Corvette is not a cut-down convertible. It is a true-blooded, tiger-tempered sports car in the noblest tradition.

Whip-lash acceleration, cat-sure cornering and handling are matched with positive safety braking and the vivid luxury of its saddle-stitched bucket seats. Brilliant styling and *color* . . . flashing, jewel-like color contrasts of cockpit and body, cowl and top make an irresistible bid for attention and approval. Surely, Corvette will be the most envied car in any setting!

Fuel Injection: One HP per Cubic Inch

In 1957 the Corvette was introduced with fuel injection. The V8 was available in two variations—with 250 and 283 HP. At the same time, a four-speed manual transmission was offered. A new era in the history of the "only American sports car" began.

Below: From the collection of scholar Ralph Brown comes this 1957 brochure. For the first time, it includes information on the new fuel injection motor.

Right: Title page of a 1959 brochure. The illustrations are racier, the sales figures better.

CHEVROLET'S NEW CORVETTE

FUN!

Ralph Brown

INTRODUCING
SENSATIONAL **NEW**
FUEL INJECTION

The new Corvette has taken a giant stride forward in 1957 with the introduction of new Ramjet Fuel Injection—the most advanced performance feature ever offered on an American production engine. Basically, Ramjet Fuel Injection is an efficient constant flow system that eliminates the carburetor, delivering fuel directly to the cylinders for instantaneous accelerator response, greater overall fuel economy, higher low-speed torque and smoothness, ease of starting and overall improvement of engine performance.

It's an extraordinary engineering feat, but the real story of Ramjet Fuel Injection is the new adventure it offers those who simply love to drive. In one bold stroke the Chevrolet Corvette now provides a new dimension of driving pleasure.

FOR THE FIRST TIME
IN AUTOMOBILE HISTORY—
ONE H.P. FOR EVERY CUBIC INCH!

Now with Fuel Injection, the 283-h.p. senior engine in the Corvette line has attained a milestone in American automotive history—one horsepower for every cubic inch. In fact, all four Corvette engines have been increased to 283 cubic inches of displacement.

The other three basic Corvette engines are the standard 220 h.p. V8, the 245 h.p. twin four-barrel V8 and the 250 h.p. V8 with Fuel Injection. Standard equipment with the Corvette is a special

3-speed close ratio transmission. (And it's a real joy to run through the gears and feel the Corvette's new snap and surge as it pours out its power.) Also, in tailoring the Corvette to individual taste, a special version of the smooth Powerglide transmission is available as an extra-cost option with certain engines. In any combination, the Corvette driver commands the most remarkable road car in America—and a show-stopper for looks, luxury and comfort.

Chevrolet

CORVETTE

AMERICA'S
SPORTS CAR

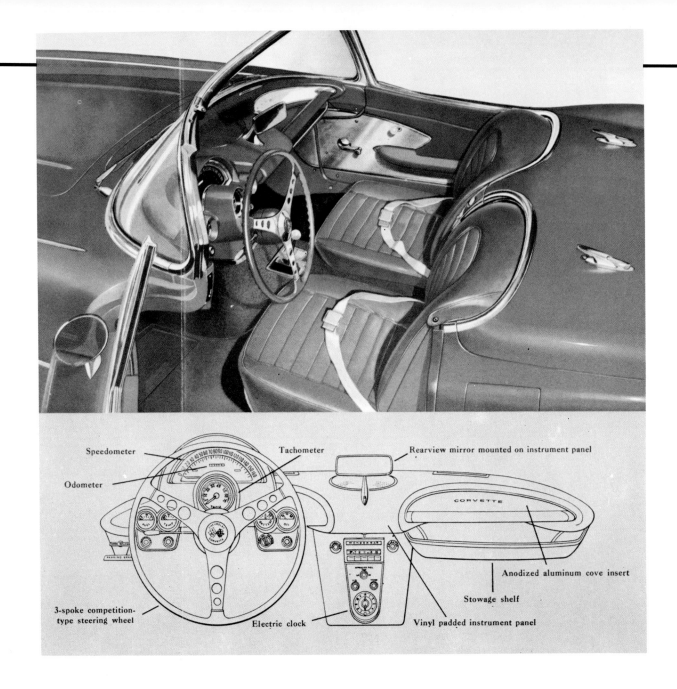

Speedometer

Tachometer

Rearview mirror mounted on instrument panel

Odometer

CORVETTE

Anodized aluminum cove insert

Stowage shelf

3-spoke competition-
type steering wheel

Electric clock

Vinyl padded instrument panel

Left: Interior shot, 1959. Right: a 1960 brochure.

CORVETTE! AMERICA'S SPORTS CAR

DESIGNED FOR PERSONAL SPORTS CAR COMFORT

CORVETTE

CORVETTE '61
BY CHEVROLET

Pictures from a test course are included in this 1961 brochure. Acceleration or other "speed" data are not included. What concerned the buyer can still be recognized clearly. The gentlemen in the car must have had a lot of fun . . .

1961

NEW CORVETTE

Above: the first Sting Ray
brochure from 1963. Motors to 360
HP are available.

new lines
new leap

FOR AMERICA'S SPORTS CAR

The '62 Corvette is many cars. To some, it is a luxurious personal form of transportation. To others, it is a machine for fun-driving endeavors—rallies, trials and gymkhanas. To still others, it is a fierce, hairy-chested fire-breather that just won't quit.

There's a spirit of fresh adventure in the '62 Corvette's lines. A new black anodized aluminum screen is set deeply in the grille. On the side, a raised windsplit completely encloses the cove, and a new rocker molding highlights Corvette's bold lines.

And, when you talk performance, you've got to talk Corvette! Four new Corvette V8s—all 327-cubic-inch engines—from 250 to 360 hp! These are hustlers that won't take a back seat to anybody! Team any of them up with Corvette's 4-speed transmission* for maximum driving flexibility. Stand on it in low—even the 250-hp "street engine" gets off the mark right now! Stand on the brakes, too. Massive stopping power matches the blistering acceleration. Then point Corvette into a corner. Its unique suspension gives you confidence. When you point it in a direction, it **GOES** in that direction and **STAYS** there.

It adds up to this: If you yearn to have a car that asks to be driven, that pampers you in luxury, that you want just for the sake of owning a fine, obedient road car, then Corvette is for you.   *Optional at extra cost.

Left: The Corvette's cockpit has been cleaned out noticeably (1965).

Above: A short rear panel for the 1962 model year. A young dream couple demonstrates on bright-colored pages how beautiful life can be on board a Corvette.

The Sting Ray was essentially more angular inbody design than its forerunner. But the new style—a Bill Mitchell creation—made a good impression. 10,919 convertibles and 10,594 coupes were produced in the 1963 model year. Later, to be sure, there was a clear preference for the open car.

Corvette Sting Ray Sport Coupe in Sebring Silver*

Corvette Sting Ray Convertible in Riverside Red with Matching Hard Top

Corvette Sting Ray Convertible in Riverside Red with White Soft Top

Corvette Sting Ray Convertible in Riverside Red

Advertising for the 1963 Sting Ray. The car can be had as a fastback coupe, a convertible with soft or hardtop. The designer Arkus-Duntov came close to many Americans' conceptions of a modern sports car with this new styling.

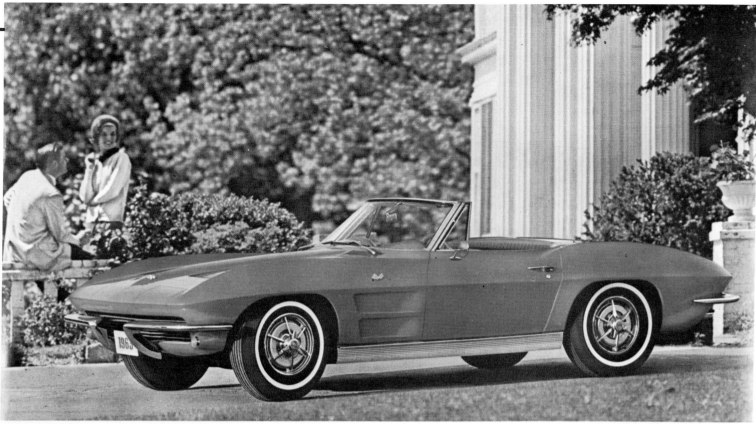

Shown on Cover: Corvette Sting Ray Sport Coupe in Riverside Red

Corvette Sting Ray Convertible in Riverside Red

NEW GRACE
AND ELEGANCE
SILHOUETTE
AMERICA'S SPORTS CAR

Corvette steps out smartly with an exhilarating new look for '63. A freshly elegant look that promises to lift the spirits of any buff who takes the wheel. It's the Corvette Sting Ray! Two sparkling new models, both pointing the way to a classic new concept in American sports car design.

Catch an eyeful of the Corvette newcomer, the exciting Sport Coupe. Graceful body panels and compound-curved side windows emphasize the miles-ahead aerodynamic design. Power-operated, retractable headlamps rotate out of sight to blend into the unobstructed hood line. Doors extend upward into the roof, adding armchair ease and comfort to sliding in and out. This is the Corvette Sting Ray Sport Coupe. Clean, taut, fresh in every detail.

You'll find the Convertible is jauntier than ever in '63. Uncluttered lines accented front and rear by trim wrap-around bumpers. The subtle contour of the smoothly molded rear deck. A gleaming aluminum grille, retractable headlamps and a sweeping hood-length windsplit. Top up or down, graceful streamlining is the goal. And the Corvette Sting Ray Convertible achieves it.

SURE-FOOTED CONFIDENCE ON THE TOUGHEST TRAILS

Two chassis innovations take much of the credit for the new Corvette's firm level ride, precise handling and maneuverability: a shorter 98" wheelbase and a unique rear suspension and newly designed rear axle. The rear suspension features a three-link independent system at each wheel. A radius arm running from the frame to the rear spindle support, a control rod attached to the differential and wheel spindle, and the double universal-jointed tubular axle shaft combine to provide nearly vertical wheel movement. One multi-leaf transverse spring (bolted to the differential carrier) extends from rear wheel to rear wheel and takes only vertical suspension loads. Braking, acceleration and lateral forces are transmitted by the radius arms, axles and control rods to the differential and the frame. The differential assembly is attached to the frame by a bolted-in crossmember; large rubber cups serve to dampen driveline vibrations. Small movements of the differential are taken up by universal joints on the one-piece propeller shaft. Corvette's new rear suspension in combination with improved coil-spring spherical joint front suspension produces better traction, a stable ride and excellent handling. You can add to tire and handling stability with Corvette's optional wide-rim cast aluminum wheels*. Vented-fin design for cooling; knock-off hubs for quick, simple wheel and tire changing.

For increased rigidity and protection, the Convertible has a steel framework surrounding the passenger compartment, while the Sport Coupe has overhead steel roof members as well.

Optional Aluminum Wheels with Knock-off Hubs.*

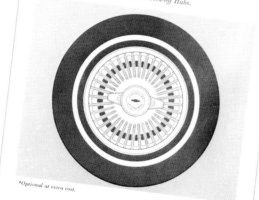

*Optional at extra cost.

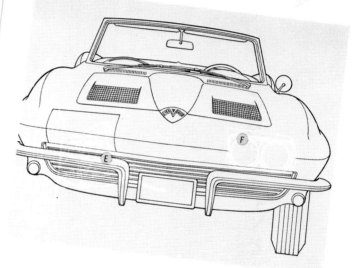

Light metal rims with central hubcaps—the newest fad. With shortened wheelbase and new rear axle, G.M. promises a completely new feeling of driving. **Right: the first 1965 brochure.**

32

1965
CORVETTE
STING RAY

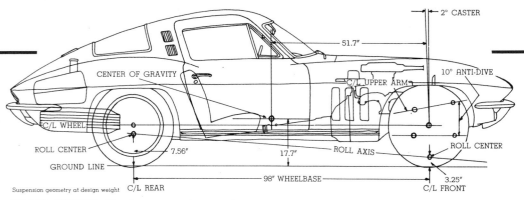

2° CASTER

51.7"

CENTER OF GRAVITY

C/L UPPER ARM

10° ANTI-DIVE

C/L WHEEL

ROLL CENTER

ROLL CENTER

GROUND LINE

7.56"

17.7"

ROLL AXIS

98" WHEELBASE

3.25"

Suspension geometry at design weight   C/L REAR

C/L FRONT

DESIGN CONCEPT: The key to Sting Ray's roadability and handling lies in its 4-wheel independent suspension and its greater rearward weight distribution. Chevrolet engineers chose the fully independent suspension so that optimum use could be made of the great power available. The rearward weight distribution makes it possible to achieve excellent handling and still maintain an acceptably gentle ride. The major vehicle masses — the heavier components of the Sting Ray — are located so that the suspension and steering systems can work with the design, rather than having to compensate for imbalance. The Sting Ray has been basically *right* from its original concept. Constant refinement and continual development have gone forward to make the 1965 Corvette Sting Ray more than ever one of

the most deeply satisfying driving experiences available in the world.

EXTRA-COST OPTIONAL EQUIPMENT

The following equipment, shown previously in illustrations or described in the text, is available at extra cost for the Corvette Sting Ray. These options add driving pleasure, or prepare the car for special uses. They allow the Sting Ray owner to equip his car to his own particular tastes.

CHASSIS: Heavy-duty suspension. (Rear spring rate: 305 lb./in. Rear shock absorbers: 1⅜ in. Front spring rate: 550 lb./in. Front shock absorbers: recalibrated. Stabilizer bar: 0.94-inch diameter.) Positraction; power brakes; telescopic steering column; power steering; optional axle ratio; nylon tires; whitewall tires; cast aluminum wheels with wide-base six-inch rims and knock-off hubs.

ENGINE: Off-road service exhaust system; exposed, side-mounted exhaust system; 36-gallon fuel tank (Sport Coupe only). (Note: when 36-gallon fuel tank is fitted, luggage compartment is partially carpeted); transistor ignition and voltage regulator; 300-horsepower engine; 350-horsepower engine; 365-horsepower engine; 375-horsepower Ramjet Fuel Injection engine.

TRANSMISSION: 4-Speed; 4-Speed close ratio; Powerglide.

BODY: Soft-Ray tinted glass; back-up lights and non-glare inside rearview mirror; Four-Season air con-

ditioning; genuine leather seat upholstery; wood-rimmed steering wheel; electric windows; AM/FM pushbutton radio with remote control power antenna; removeable hard top. (Convertible only. You can, however, specify either hard top or soft top at no extra cost—or order both with hard top at extra cost.)

Gas filler door emblem

from rubber to roof, a sports car...

for performance -and style-minded individuals.

Pictures from a 1965 brochure. It includes excellent photos and detailed drawings.

The body of the '65
Corvette consists,
the catalog says, of
31 plastic pieces.
Right: Picture from
a 1966 brochure.

The sport coupe's fully carpeted luggage area
Right: Enthusiast's delight: 4-Speed box
Seat belts with retractors are standard

Pushbutton AM/FM all-transistor radio

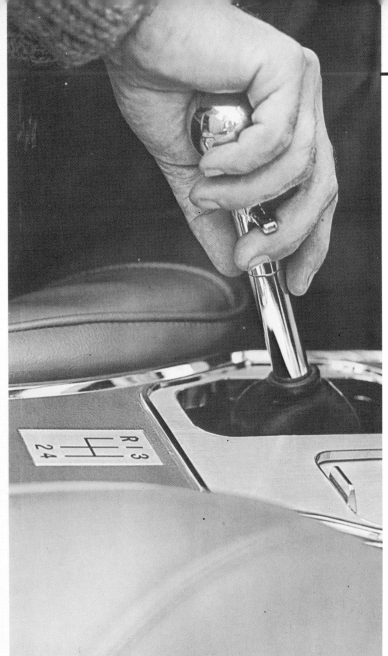

Manual shifting is considered sporting, but an automatic transmission was also available. And two-point seat belts were still considered satisfactory.

Lively drawings in this '67 Corvette brochure proclaim new features. A combination of ten body colors and 8 interior variations is offered.

'67 Corvette
BY CHEVROLET

energetic

By definition, energy is "internal power with the capacity of acting." You can define the kind of energetic action you want in your Corvette with the help of an expanded lineup of V8s for '67, backed by three transmissions and five rear axle ratios.

The big attraction for Corvette fanciers is the change that's come over the 427 Turbo-Jets. Now there are three of these top-performing 427-cu.-in. engines under a special bubble hood — two of them brand-new and equipped with three 2-barrel carburetors in a row. Highest rated member of this trio is the 435-hp version which features mechanical valve lifters and a special-performance camshaft. It has a compression ratio of 11.0:1.

The 400-hp 427 also features triple 2-barrel carburetion but uses hydraulic lifters and a high-performance camshaft for quiet operation. Finally, there's a 390-hp 427 Turbo-Jet with 4-barrel carb, hydraulic lifters and high-performance cam. These two 427s have a 10.25:1 compression ratio.

Special features make the three 427 Turbo-Jet engines extremely durable and efficient. To name a few: extra-wide-base main bearing caps that add to the support of each of the five main bearings; premium aluminum main and connecting rod bearings plus construction which produces extended durability; big valves that help cylinder heads breathe quickly and freely; individual intake and exhaust ports plus other refinements all help to increase the volume of combustibles and improve exhausting.

All 427 V8s are bored to 4.251 inches and travel through a 3.76-inch stroke. Combustion chambers are of modified-wedge design. Resulting forces of combustion react more to push the piston down rather than heat the sidewalls of the chamber.

Standard engine in a '67 Corvette is the 300-hp 327-cu.-in. V8. And if you need more, you can order the 350-hp version of the same 327 block. The 300-hp engine utilizes a general-performance cam and has a compression ratio of 10.0:1; the heftier

327 V8 has a high-performance camshaft, 4-barrel carburetor with special aluminum intake manifold and an 11.0:1 compression ratio. Both have hydraulic valve lifters.

Oil capacity for the standard Corvette engine is five quarts — filter included. For the extra-cost engines, six quarts of oil are required with filter.

For the '67 Corvette, a 3-Speed fully synchronized gearbox is coupled with the 300-hp 327-cu.-in. engine as standard equipment. A 4-Speed with 2.52:1 ratio 1st gear may be ordered with 300-, 350-, 390- or 400-hp engines; a 2.20:1 ratio 1st gear 4-Speed may be specified with 350-, 390-,

400- and 435-hp V8s. This year, for more leisure-minded sports car buffs, Powerglide automatic transmission can be ordered with the 300-, 390-, and 400-hp engines.

Five rear axle ratios are available, depending on the engine you select, to provide you with smooth going or rugged performance. A Positraction rear axle, which can be specified with any Corvette ratio, routes engine power to the rear wheel with the greatest traction. This is especially valuable on muddy, slippery or other irregular surfaces, in sand and snow. Check the axle ratio chart at right to determine rate of speed with various axle ratios.

MILES PER HOUR PER 1000 ENGINE RPM IN FINAL DRIVE	
(Figures are estimated without allowance for tire expansion or slippage.)	
3.08:1 = 25.6	3.36:1 = 23.1
3.55:1 = 22.2	3.70:1 = 21.3
4.11:1 = 19.2	

Try a '67 Corvette as soon as you can. You'll find there's no energy wasted.

EXTRA-COST OPTIONS AND CUSTOM FEATURES* TO MAKE DRIVING A CORVETTE EVEN MORE PLEASURABLE

350-hp Turbo-Fire 327; 390-, 400- or 435-hp Turbo-Jet 427. An automatic Powerglide or 4-Speed fully synchronized transmission. Four-Season air conditioning. Power brakes, power steering, power windows. AM/FM pushbutton radio. Removable hardtop for convertible. Black vinyl roof cover for removable hardtop. Positraction rear axle. Leather seat trim. Shoulder belts. White-wall or red-stripe tires. Soft-Ray tinted windows and/or windshield. Full-transistor ignition system (not available with standard engine). Heavy-duty brakes. Special-performance front and rear suspension. Off-road exhaust system (not available with Powerglide). Dual side-mounted off-road exhausts. Telescopic steering wheel. Emergency road kit. Compass. Gas tank filler cap lock. Removable floor mats. 36.5-gallon gas tank for sport coupe only. Convertible deck lid luggage carrier plus strap. Convertible deck lid ski rack. Strato-ease headrests. Speed warning unit. Portable hand spotlight. Special cast-aluminum wheels.

*Check your Chevrolet dealer for these and other extra-cost items along with their model application and availability with other equipment.

9

1967 STING RAY POWER TEAMS

Engine Bore & Stroke	Horsepower & Torque at RPM	Carburetion & Induction System	Comp. Ratio	Cam & Lifters	Trans-missions	Axle Ratios	
						Standard	Positraction
STANDARD ENGINE							
327-cu.-in. V8	300 @ 5000	4-Barrel	10.0:1	General Performance	3-Speed (2.54:1 Low)	3.36:1	3.08:1
4.00 x 3.25 ins.	360 @ 3400	High-Flow Air Cleaner		Hydraulic	4-Speed (2.52:1 Low)	3.36:1	3.08:1 3.36:1
					Powerglide	3.36:1	3.36:1
EXTRA-COST OPTIONAL ENGINES							
327-cu.-in. V8	350 @ 5800	4-Barrel	11.0:1	High Performance	4-Speed (2.52:1 Low)	3.36:1	3.36:1 3.55:1
4.00 x 3.25 ins.	360 @ 3600	High-Flow Air Cleaner		Hydraulic	4-Speed (2.20:1 Low)	3.70:1	3.70:1 4.11:1
427-cu.-in. V8	390 @ 5400	4-Barrel	10.25:1	High Performance	4-Speed (2.52:1 Low)	3.08:1*	3.36:1
4.251 x 3.76 ins.	460 @ 3600	High-Flow Air Cleaner		Hydraulic	4-Speed (2.20:1 Low)	3.36:1*	3.08:1 3.55:1
					Powerglide	3.36:1*	3.70:1
427-cu.-in. V8	400 @ 5400	Triple 2-Barrel	10.25:1	High Performance	4-Speed (2.52:1 Low)	3.08:1*	3.36:1
4.251 x 3.76 ins.	460 @ 3600	High-Flow Air Cleaner		Hydraulic	4-Speed (2.20:1 Low)	3.36:1*	3.08:1 3.55:1 3.70:1
					Powerglide		
427-cu.-in. V8	435 @ 5800	Triple 2-Barrel	11.0:1	Special Performance	4-Speed (2.20:1 Low)	3.55:1*	3.36:1* 3.70:1*
4.251 x 3.76 ins.	460 @ 4000	High-Flow Air Cleaner		Mechanical			4.11:1*

*Available as Positraction only

Motor variations that left no wishes unfulfilled, and corresponding gearbox and rear-axle types. The extra prices for such extras were modest . . .

Left: Title page of the first brochure for the 1968 model year. The car, completely reworked inside and out, looks extremely bullish, if not aggressive. Three-point belts are now standard in the coupe.

Right: There are many other new details, including the recessed windshield wipers or the ventilation system. The press described the Corvette as "the best all-round car" of the year—for the fourth time. The illustrations on the following pages come from the same catalog.

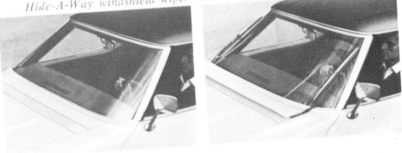

Hide-A-Way windshield wiper-washer system closed . . . and open.

For comfort, air flows through Corvette with full door windows closed, thanks to the new Astro Ventilation system with vent-ports in the driver and passenger sides of the instrument panel. For protection, there are safety features like never before (some are listed on page 11). For long-lasting good looks, choose from ten Magic-Mirror finishes. Corvette '68 . . . all different all over.

43

Corvette Sting Ray Coupe interior with high-back slim-tapered bucket seats.

Settle down!

The Corvette cockpit is made for the traveling duo. Thin tapered and contoured buckets are very comfortably high-backed. Supple all-vinyl upholstery is standard, or you can order genuine leather. Between the seats the center console houses the parking brake lever, gear shift, cigarette lighter and ashtray, thumb-wheel heater controls, air vent controls, and light monitoring system indicators (to check operation of important outside running lights from inside through space-age fiber optics). The console also stows seat belt buckle straps—twin sets with pushbutton buckles are standard. Coupe equipment also includes twin shoulder belts.

Riding just above the console is the recessed instrument cluster. Here's where the engine tale is told. Water temperature, oil pressure and fuel gauges along with an ammeter and rally clock are positioned for easy reading. Windshield wiper-washer controls are also in console. And if you order an AM/FM radio—available with or without FM Stereo multiplex—controls are mounted here horizontally. Joining in are new features like door ajar flasher and seat belt reminder light. Directly in front of the driver are the speedometer, tachometer, trip odometer, light controls, ignition lock, high beam indicator, turn signal indicator, brake system warning light—and a 3-spoke steering wheel that looks like wood.

Luxurious deep-twist carpeting looks and feels great. It even

6

44

Go hardtop!

The Corvette Sting Ray is for those who appreciate the true sports kind of car — and even for those who don't right now. It's that special kind of an automobile that comes along about once every generation to totally arrest the imagination of car buffs. In 15 years of Corvettes the car has not only driven into prominence in the sports car field, but has also been a forerunner of some exciting and practical automobile innovation. For 1968, the mechanics of Sting Ray have been improved and refined (it's still basically made for people who feel that the best part of living is driving), and this, obviously, is a most inspiring year for design.

Consider: the '68 Sting Ray Coupe is a hardtop and more. Uncommon removable sections over pilot and navigator lift out for open air moving. A nearly vertical glass rear window tucks out of the way into a neat compartment in the luggage area. The effect is a flow-through cochère roof that's never been seen on an American production sports car until now.

Long, low profile with blunt styling brings up the rear per the continental GT tradition. The aerodynamic design features a spoiler back there, too. Behind front wheels, functional louvers help keep the horses cool. Wraparound front and rear bumpers plus line-smoothing hideaway features help make Corvette a trim one style-wise. On the nose end, vacuum-operated headlights glide open automatically when lights are turned on. Windshield wipers aren't around when they shouldn't be. They're hidden under a power-operated panel which actuates when

1969 CORVETTE

Putting you first, keeps us first  CHEVROLET

Title page of the new brochure for 1969 and an interior shot. Studio
tricks and brilliant close-ups take turns (following pages).

grabbing 15-inch wide ovals plus new 8-inch wide wheels and wider tread give Stingray a better grip . . . and an even bolder appearance. Other subtle but significant refine-

ments include a stronger, more rigid frame for improved ride and handling, new maximum security 3-way locking system on the steering column and unique headlight

washers that even clean in motion with jets of water.

Shown here are the ways you can get it: Coupe with removable hardtop sections; Convertible with soft top or

removable hardtop. *For a more complete list of Corvette extra-cost Options and Custom Features illustrated or described throughout this book, see Page 11.*

Convertible with top down.

Vinyl-covered removable hardtop.

Headlight washers.

CORVETTE

48

V8's in addition to the standard 300-hp V8. Prefer 4-Speed? You have a choice of gear ratios offered with all engines except the standard 300-hp and the 435-hp V8.

New Corvette power team features for '69 include new, larger 350 CID 300-hp engine as standard, or a 350-hp version is available, sturdier engine construction on the 350 CID, thicker bulkheads and main bearing caps, firmer crankshaft clamping with longer washer head bolts, extra-firm 4-bolt main bearing cap attachment and improved cooling system.

We even have a special engine (L-88) that we don't recommend for street use.

Transmissions: Standard 3-Speed fully synchronized; 4-Speed fully synchronized (wide-range or close-ratio); Turbo Hydra-Matic which operates automatically unless you want to shift it—through three forward ranges.

Of course, four-wheel disc brakes are still standard on Corvette—and in stopping ability, fade resistance and modulation they're very much appreciated by just about anybody interested in sports cars. Other features you get with Corvette include a new anti-interference ignition system, a high-output Delcotron generator, high-capacity energizer type battery, rustproof fiber glass body—and everything put together with a thoroughness and attention to detail that Corvette owners fully understand.

Standard equipment safety and security features on the 1969 Corvette include: energy-absorbing steering column □ seat belts with pushbutton buckles □ shoulder belts with inertia retractors (Coupe only) □ head restraints □ passenger-guard door locks □ safety door latches and hinges □ four-way hazard warning flasher □ dual master cylinder brake system with warning light and corrosion-resistant brake lines □ tire safety rims □ folding seat back latches □ dual-speed windshield wipers and washer □ dual-action safety hood latch □ outside rearview mirror □ back-up lights □ side marker lights and parking lights that illuminate with headlights □ energy-absorbing instrument panel □ padded sun visors □ reduced-glare instrument panel top, inside windshield mouldings, steering wheel hub and windshield wiper arms and blades □ wide inside day-night mirror with deflecting base □ lane-change feature in direction signal control □ safety armrests □ thick-laminate windshield □ soft, low-profile window control knobs □ smooth contoured door and window regulator handles □ anti-theft ignition key warning buzzer □ starter safety switch (to prevent engine starting when in gear) on all transmissions □ snag-resistant steering wheel hardware □ non-projecting wheel trim □ improved fuel tank retention □ headlight aiming access provision □ fail-safe concealed headlights □ anti-theft ignition, steering and transmission lock.

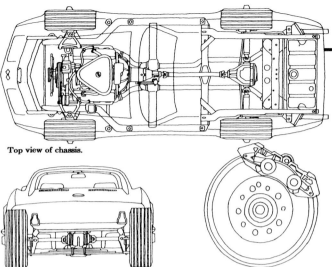

Top view of chassis.

Fully independent rear suspension.

Advanced design disc brakes.

		Rear Axle Ratio (:1)							
		Without Air Cond.				With Air Cond.			
Engine	Transmission	Std	Optional Econ	Optional Perf	Optional Spcl	Std	Optional Econ	Optional Perf	Optional Spcl
BASE ENGINE									
300 HP Turbo-Fire 350 350-Cu.-In. V8	3-Speed (2.54:1 Low)	3.36*	3.08**			3.36*	3.08**		
	4-Speed (2.52:1 Low)								
	Turbo Hydra-Matic	3.08**				3.08**			
OPTIONAL ENGINES									
350 HP Turbo-Fire 350 350-Cu.-In. V8 RPO L46	4-Speed (2.52:1 Low)	3.36*		3.55**		3.36*		3.55**	
	4-Speed (2.20:1 Low)	3.70*		4.11**		3.70*		4.11**	
390 HP Turbo-Jet 427 427-Cu.-In. V8 RPO L36	4-Speed (2.52:1 Low)	3.08**		3.36**		3.08**			
	4-Speed (2.20:1 Low)	3.36**	3.08**	3.55**	3.70**	Air Conditioning Not Available			
	Turbo Hydra-Matic	3.08**	2.73**			3.08**	2.73**		
400 HP Turbo-Jet 427 427-Cu.-In. V8 RPO L68	4-Speed (2.52:1 Low)	3.08**		3.36**		3.08**			
	4-Speed (2.20:1 Low)	3.36**	3.08**	3.55**	3.70**	Air Conditioning Not Available			
	Turbo Hydra-Matic	3.08**	2.73**			3.08**	2.73**		
435 HP Turbo-Jet 427 427-Cu.-In. V8 RPO L71	4-Speed (2.20:1 Low)	3.55**	3.36**	3.70**	4.11**	Air Conditioning Not Available			
	Turbo Hydra-Matic	3.08**	2.73**	3.36**		Air Conditioning Not Available			
SPECIAL HIGH PERFORMANCE ENGINE (OFF-ROAD APPLICATION ONLY)									
430 HP Turbo-Jet 427 427-Cu.-In. V8 RPO L88	H.D. 4-Speed (2.20:1 Low)	3.36**	3.08**	3.55**	3.70 4.11 4.56**	Air Conditioning Not Available			
	Turbo Hydra-Matic	3.08**	2.73**	3.36**		Air Conditioning Not Available			

*Positraction available.   **Positraction required.

Corvette Stingray Coupe

CHEVROLET

Litho in U.S.A.—D-67141

GM
MARK OF EXCELLENCE

Corvette pioneered. It hasn't stopped. When Chevrolet introduces something new—from disc brakes to a hidden headlight system—it usually debuts on Corvette.

You buy an environment. It's an automobile, sure, but you'll find yourself knowing more about it than anything you've ever driven. It's got gauges galore for the ultimate in feedback.

Buy any other sports car and all you get is today's car. Buy a Corvette and you buy a piece of tomorrow.

Left: 1969 advertising—with a lot of black magic. Right: In 1970 it was suggested that one got more than just a car when one bought a Corvette. Did they mean the lady in the background?

YNJ 037

Many of the items pictured on these cars are extra-cost Options and Custom Features. For a complete listing, see your dealer.
Copyright 1970, Chevrolet Motor Division, General Motors Corporation

Mission Control Center '70.

Cape Kennedy hasn't got anything on us. Corvette's cockpit is as heavy on instrumentation as it is on comfort.

First, you sit yourself down in one of the high-backed contoured bucket seats featuring our new integrated head restraints. The shoulder belts (standard on coupe) are guided through a slot in each seatback for neat, secure positioning.

You rest your feet on soft carpeting that not only stretches wall to wall but over the entire rear stowage

area with its hidden compartments for valuables, battery and tools.

You check out the central command console before your countdown. Tach, ammeter, water temp, oil pressure, fuel gauge, brake warning light, running light monitors—you name it, it's there.

Once under way, you can enjoy Astro Ventilation, which routes outside air in, through your choice of high or low vents. A rear deck vent exhausts stale air,

for a constant flow, even with the windows closed.

New for '70 is a Custom Interior you can order with black or saddle leather seats, plush cut-pile carpeting and the rich look of wood on door panels and console.

The standard all-vinyl interior comes in black, saddle, dark brown, dark green, blue and red.

No matter if your mission's only a trip to the drive-in, the interior of the 1970 Corvette is designed to put you in complete control.

Left: Interior view from the 1970 Corvette brochure. **Right:** strength in numbers—425 **SAE HP** are offered. **The** car is deliberately shown on an (empty) racetrack.

Chevrolet Corvette Custom Interior and Tilt-Telescopic steering column.

Strength in numbers for 1971- 270, 330, 365, 425 hp.

Every Corvette is built tough right from the start. Our basic V8, the 270-hp Turbo-Fire 350, features an 8.5:1 compression ratio, a 4-barrel carb, cast aluminum alloy pistons and a precision-formed crank. With this, and all other Corvette engines, you get Corvette's dual exhausts with rectangular outlets and Positraction differential standard.

Go one step up to the 330-hp Turbo-Fire 350, and you get a 9.0:1 compression ratio, impact-extruded aluminum alloy pistons, finned aluminum rocker covers, a special-performance cam, mechanical lifters and a forged steel-alloy crank. Plus an aluminum intake manifold, high-domed hood, transistor ignition.

Next step up. Our 365-hp 454-cu.-in. Turbo-Jet V8. This engine with 8.5:1 compression ratio uses a dual-snorkel air cleaner with a chromed cover and an extra-large oil pan. You also get a high-domed hood, a larger diameter front stabilizer bar, heavier duty rear wheel spindle support arms, a rear suspension stabilizer bar, a larger capacity radiator, dual pulleys for the fan and water pump

and a higher performance starter motor.

Also available: our 425-hp Turbo-Jet 454 with a large 4-barrel carb, high-performance cam, mechanical lifters, 9.0:1 compression ratio and aluminum cylinder heads. Plus chassis items included with the 365-hp V8.

Transmissions: standard gearbox is a floor-mounted, wide-range 4-Speed, 2.52:1 low gear. Also available, a close-ratio version with a 2.20:1 low (close ratio not available with 270-hp engine, wide range not available with 425-hp engine). A Special 4-Speed close ratio box is available with the 425-hp V8.

With the 270-, 365-, and 425-hp engines, you can order Turbo Hydra-matic.

Chevrolet Corvette Stingray Convertible with removable hardtop.

1973 CORVETTE
Building a better way to see the U.S.A.

STINGRAY COUPE/STINGRAY CONVERTIBLE

Chevrolet

Pictures from a 1973 catalog. Note that "Stingray" is no longer written in two words.

The Corvette Stingray Convertible
makes being under the weather a
pleasure. All you have to do with the
folding top is unlatch it, raise it, drop it,
snap it and forget it. The deck cover
covers it all. Top available in both
black and white.

You can also order a removable hardtop. It's well worth having. For winter,
for variety and for saving your
folding top for a sunny day.

The Corvette Instrument Panel is
more like a cockpit than a dashboard.
Left to right: a big speedometer and an
equally big tachometer. The five other
gauges tell you the coolant temperature,
oil pressure, amperage, fuel level and
the time. Above the gauges on the console, controls for the windshield washers
and wipers. Below, heating and venti-
lating controls. Within easy reach is the
AM/FM radio or AM/FM/Stereo radio
you can order. With one speaker for
you. And one for your co-pilot.

The Standard Corvette Interior is up
to pretty high standards.
The high-backed contoured bucket
seats are virtually handmade. They're
cushioned with thick foam and have
built-in head restraints. Fold either seat
forward and you're into Corvette's
fully carpeted, illuminated luggage
area. Two storage compartments are
concealed behind the seats. A third
compartment conceals the battery. The
remainder of the passenger area is
trimmed in rich padded vinyl with deep
twist carpeting on the floor. Available
in black, blue, medium saddle, dark
saddle and red.

**The Available Custom Corvette
Interior** (shown at left). The seat panels
are genuine leather with matching
vinyl trim. There are wood-grained
vinyl accents on the doors and console.
Underfoot, deep cut-pile nylon carpeting. You're literally riding in the lap
of luxury. Black, medium saddle or
dark saddle.

BUILDING A BETTER WAY TO SEE THE U.S.A.   Chevrolet

OPTIONS

1974 Corvette advertising— quite a change. Photos and light water colors give an unusual contrast. In small print it is mentioned that one can also have leather seats.

FOR THE BODY

Removable Hardtop (for convertible)—The way to give your convertible top a vacation during cold weather. And yourself the added warmth and quiet of a hardtop. It's styled to enhance the lines of the Corvette and can be ordered to match the exterior color, or with an available black vinyl roof cover for a more formal look.

Luggage Rack (dealer-installed)—It's handsome enough to be strictly a dress-up item. But isn't it nice that it also lets you store the occasional overflow from your luggage compartment?

Also Available (from your dealer)— • Right-hand outside mirror • Non-vented locking gas cap.

FOR THE CHASSIS

Turbo-Fire 350-4 Special V8—When we say that we've given this 350 a special carb, cam, crank, cylinder heads, pistons, rods, even finned aluminum rocker arm covers, we still haven't said it all. Designed to come on in the higher RPM numbers, the Special is obviously an engine for the enthusiast.

Turbo-Jet 454-4 V8—Like they say: "Nothing beats inches." And with 454 cubic inches of displacement, the Turbo-Jet provides a lusty torque output over the entire RPM operating range. This engine, like all 1974 Corvette engines, features a new multi-louvered radiator for improved cooling in city traffic conditions.

Console-Shift Turbo Hydra-matic Transmission—Think of this automatic three-speed as a box with a dual personality. Leave it in "Drive" range when you've got other things on your mind. Shift it manually with the console T-handle when special acceleration or engine braking needs are called for. Available with all engines.

Close-Ratio 4-Speed Manual Transmission—Fully synchronized with a 2.20:1 first gear ratio, this gearbox provides

The choice.

Buy a Corvette and you say a lot about yourself. Say more by the available equipment you order.

FOR COMFORT, CONVENIENCE, APPEARANCE.

• New glass canopy roof panels. Deep tint reduces sun glare.
• Electro-Clear rear window defogger with control switch and warning light on console.
• Four-Season air conditioning. Especially desirable when you're driving Corvette buttoned up on hot, humid days or nights.
• Delco sound systems. Featured are dual speakers selected to match the acoustics of the Corvette interior. Your choice of AM/FM monaural radio, AM/FM stereo radio or (new for '77) AM/FM stereo radio with stereo 8-track tape player.
• Tilt-Telescopic steering wheel. Adjusts to six different angles, also includes telescopic travel for different driving positions, easier exiting and entering. Includes new leather-wrapped,

three-spoke sport steering wheel (shown on front cover).
• Cruise-Master speed control. Set to hold desired speed.
• Sport mirrors. Twin outside rearview mirrors in body-color pods. Driver's side is remote-controlled; passenger's side is convex.
• Bright-finish rear deck luggage carrier. For '77, has provisions for stowing roof panels.

• Power windows.
• Floor mats with multi-color carpet inserts.
• GR70 white lettered steel-belted radial ply tires.
• Special 15" x 8" cast aluminum wheels (4) with fifth steel wheel for spare.
• Convenience package. Includes momentary stay-lit feature for dome and courtesy lights, visor mirror, "headlights on" buzzer, low fuel indicator and engine compartment light.

MECHANICAL ITEMS.

• Special 350 4-barrel V8 (L82). Features a higher lift cam than the standard 350 V8, special heads with larger valves, impact-extruded pistons, a forged crank running in 4-bolt main bearing caps, plus finned aluminum rocker arm covers.
• Close-ratio 4-Speed manual transmission. The close ratios of this 4-Speed are better suited for numerous high-speed up-and-down shifts associated with competition driving. Fully synchronized with a 2.43 to one first-gear ratio.
• Turbo Hydra-matic transmission. This 3-range automatic can also be shifted manually.

• Highway rear axle ratios. Lower-than-standard numerical ratios permit cruising at lower engine speeds than with standard ratio. See inside page for availability.
• Gymkhana suspension. Provides larger diameter front stabilizer bar, a rear stabilizer bar plus stiffer springs and special shock absorbers, front and rear.
• Heavy-duty Freedom battery. No add-water servicing required. 4,000-watt rating.

DEALER-INSTALLED ACCESSORIES.

• Trailering equipment available for loads up to 4,000-lb. GVW.
• Citizens Band equipment.
• Plus many more.

All illustrations and specifications contained in this literature are based on the latest product information available at the time of publication approval. The right is reserved to make changes at any time without notice in prices, colors, materials, equipment, specifications and models, and to discontinue models. Chevrolet Motor Division, General Motors Corporation, Detroit, Michigan 48202.
LITHO IN U.S.A.

3411

September, 1976

Chevrolet

Black and strong—and now with the popular T-Top!

58

This is what makes your Corvette what it is: America's only true production sports car.

ON THE OUTSIDE.

Corvette's low-slung aerodynamic styling and fiberglass body need no introduction. Also:
- Lightweight, remove-and-store roof panels convert your Corvette in seconds from closed- to open-top coupe, or vice versa. This year we've made provisions to stow the panels on the available deck-lid luggage carrier if you wish, to give more interior luggage room (see back cover).
- Energy-absorbing bumpers covered by soft, molded urethane in body color.
- Dual molded bumper guards, front and rear.
- Flush, retracting dual headlamps; dual-unit circular taillights.
- Soft-Ray tinted glass.
- Black windshield posts give new "thin pillar" look.
- 15" x 8" steel wheels with bright hub covers and trim rings.
- Hide-A-Way windshield wipers.
- New exterior colors: yellow, black, dark red, orange, dark blue, light blue metallic, tan buckskin. Continued: classic white, silver and medium red.

THE COCKPIT.

It's intimate as only a two-seater can be, yet functional as a sports car must be.
- Two-level instrumentation. Tachometer and speedometer with trip odometer are centered in front of the driver's eyes, high on the panel (just below the driver's road view) on two large circular dials. Voltmeter, coolant temperature, oil pressure, fuel level and electric clock are on a separate panel, in smaller, aircraft-styled dials, at the forward end of the console.
- Center console puts the following controls at your right hand: shift selector (with new leather boot); heating/ventilation plus ashtray and lighter. Controls for available air conditioning,

power windows, Electro-Clear rear window defogger with warning light are also located on the console. New features include a handy coin tray and a soft vinyl housing over the parking brake handle.
- Four-spoke, padded-vinyl-covered steering wheel is now positioned two inches farther from driver to ease entry and exit.
- New column-mounted "Smart Switch" puts these controls at your left hand: turn signals, hi-lo headlight beam selection, windshield wipers and washers.
- Padded sun shades now swivel to provide some glare protection from side as well as front.
- Overhead and underpanel courtesy lights actuate automatically when either door opens, or manually with headlight switch.
- Panel-mounted map pockets.
- Extensive sound insulation.
- Nylon, cut-pile, color-keyed carpeting for passenger and luggage compartment.
- Luggage compartment behind seats and two storage chambers (one lockable for valuables), featuring increased ease of access for '77.
- Now standard is custom-level interior trim, featuring choice of leather (back cover) or cloth-and-leather seating surfaces (below) on full foam, deep-contoured bucket seats. Select from black, buckskin, red, smoke gray, blue or brown. Or choose from

- Power steering.

leather-seat interiors in white with buckskin, red, smoke gray or blue accents.

THE POWER TEAM.

Get the one that best suits your personal driving preferences.
- The standard 350 4-barrel V8 is a rugged power plant with impressive low-speed torque for around-town cruising, but also very willing and responsive on the highway.
- The standard wide-ratio 4-Speed manual transmission is great for normal driving. The high numerical first-gear ratio gets you off the mark smartly, while wide-range intermediate ratios provide good torque matching at low and intermediate speeds.

Engines (5.7 Litre)	Transmissions	Rear Axle Ratios
Standard 350 4-barrel V8 Net HP*, 180 @ 4000 RPM Torque, 270 ft.-lbs. @ 2400 RPM	4-Speed, Wide Ratio, Std.†**	3.36, Std.
		3.08, Avail.
	Turbo Hydra-matic, Avail.	3.08, Std.
Available† Special 350 4-barrel V8 Net HP*, 210 @ 5200 RPM Torque, 255 ft.-lbs. @ 3600 RPM	4-Speed, Wide Ratio, Std.†**	3.70, Std.
		3.55, Avail.
	4-Speed, Close Ratio, Avail.†**	3.70, Std.
		3.55, Avail.
	Turbo Hydra-matic, Avail.	3.55, Std.

SPECIAL NOTE: California Emission Equipment required for registration in California. In other states, High Altitude Emission Equipment may be required in areas 4,000 or more feet above sea level.
*SAE net (as installed) rating.
†Not available in California.
**High Altitude Emission Equipment.

CORVETTE ENGINES HAVE:
- High Energy Ignition, a solid-state system that delivers up to 85% hotter spark to the plugs than a conventional system.
- Hydraulic valve lifters.
- Coolant recovery system to help reduce coolant loss.
- Delcotron generator with solid-

state regulator.
- Freedom battery needs no refills. Side terminals eliminate corrosion buildup. 3,500-watt rating.
- Long recommended maintenance intervals: Spark plugs, up to 22,500 miles; engine oil, 6 months or 7,500 miles; oil filter, first 7,500 miles, then every 15,000 miles; chassis lube, 6 months or 7,500 miles; automatic transmission fluid, 60,000 miles. Check details in the Owner's Manual.

FOR SAFETY AND SECURITY.

Occupant protection.
- Two combination seat and inertia reel shoulder belts for driver (with reminder light and buzzer) and right seat passenger.
- Energy-absorbing steering column.
- Safety steering wheel.
- Passenger-guard door locks.
- Safety door latches and hinges.
- Folding seat back latches.
- Energy-absorbing padded instrument panel.
- Thick-laminate windshield.
- Safety armrests.

Accident prevention.
- Side marker lights and reflectors.
- Parking lamps that illuminate with headlamps.
- Four-way hazard warning flasher.
- Lane-change feature in direction signal control.
- Backup lights.
- Windshield defrosters, washers and dual-speed wipers.
- Wide-view inside day-night mirror (vinyl-edged, shatter-resistant glass and deflecting support).
- Outside rearview mirror.
- Dual master cylinder brake system with warning light.
- Starter safety switch.

Anti-theft.
- Alarm set or deactivated by key lock in left front fender.
- Ignition-key reminder buzzer.
- Steering column lock.

The only one

Corvette by Chevrolet.

Don't miss the note that the Corvette is delivered with modified equipment in California. But as before, horsepower is not mentioned.

- Head room: 36.2".
- Shoulder room: 47.9".
- Hip room: 48.8".
- Leg room: 52.1".
- Luggage space: 7.8 cu. ft.

- Magic-Mirror acrylic exterior finish.

- Fiberglass body construction can't rust or corrode.

- Fuel tank rated capacity: 18 gals.

- New stainless steel covers on mufflers—added protection against corrosion.

- Power disc brakes at all four wheels. Fade-resistant and self-adjusting.

- Protective fiberglass inner fenders, front and rear.

- Fully independent front and rear suspension.

- Wide 15" x 8" wheels.
- Wheelbase: 98.0".
- Overall length: 185.2".
- Overall width: 69.0".
- Loaded height: 48.0".
- Tread: front—58.7", rear—59.5".

- Corvette-specification, GR70-series, steel-belted radial ply tires.

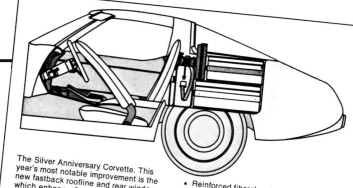

Left: This folding card appeared at the end of 1977, with the 25-year history of Corvette. At right, the specifications of that year's car.

The Silver Anniversary Corvette. This year's most notable improvement is the new fastback roofline and rear window which enhance Corvette's sleek silhouette. Additionally, the new rear window not only allows for a cleaner styling profile, it also improves driver visibility and adds luggage space. There's a roll shade to screen the luggage space. And there's room inside for storage of removable roof panels.

Also new for 1978 is a larger, plastic-lined fuel tank. Capacity has been boosted from 17 to 24 gallons.

The instrument panel has also been restyled and features face-mounted, round instruments which are extremely legible as well as handsome. A new glove box has been added, too.

Corvette performance has been improved with a dual snorkel air cleaner and new low-restriction exhaust system and mufflers on the available L82 350 Cu. In. V8 engine (not available in California). The transverse rear leaf spring in the independent rear suspension has been widened to reduce stress.

Two new transmissions are introduced in 1978. A new Four-Speed manual transmission is standard. A new automatic transmission is available for the L82 350 Cu. In. V8 engine. And in recognition of Corvette's 25th year, Silver Anniversary emblems are mounted on the nose and rear deck.

Corvette continues to offer a long list of standard equipment:
• 4-barrel 350 Cu. In. V8.
• Choice of 4-Speed manual or automatic transmission.
• Independent suspension, front and rear.
• Power steering.

• Reinforced fiberglass body construction that can't rust or corrode.
• Power disc brakes at all four wheels; self-adjusting and fade-resistant.
• Low-profile, steel-belted radial ply tires.
• Wide 15" x 8" wheels.
• Body-colored, energy-absorbing bumpers.
• Flush-mounted, retractable headlights.
• Soft-Ray tinted glass.
• Center console.
• Column-mounted switch that controls turn signals, high and low headlight beams.
• Choice of leather or cloth and leather seat inserts.
• Full foam, deep contoured bucket seats.
• Choice of 10 exterior colors, 7 interior colors.
• Carpeted floor, including tunnel sides and door sills.
• Twin bumper guards, front and rear.
• Removable roof panels.
• Automatic overhead and instrument panel courtesy lights.
• Extensive sound insulation.
• Electric clock.
• Lockable storage compartments.
• Full instrumentation, including speedometer, tachometer, water temperature gage, fuel gage, voltmeter, oil pressure gage, and trip odometer.
• Delco Freedom battery that needs no water.

• High Energy Ignition system.
• Delcotron generator with solid-state voltage regulator.
• Fiberglass inner fenders.

Long recommended service intervals under normal driving conditions.

Engine oil	12 months or 7,500 miles
Chassis lubrication	12 months or 7,500 miles
Oil filter	First 7,500 miles. Every 15,000 miles thereafter.
Spark plugs	Up to 22,500 miles
Automatic transmission fluid	60,000 miles

SAFETY FEATURES

OCCUPANT PROTECTION FEATURES
• Continuous loop seat belt and inertia reel shoulder harness for driver (with reminder light and buzzer) and passenger
• Padded sun visors • Energy-absorbing steering column • Passenger guard door locks • Safety door latches and stamped steel hinges • Folding seat-back latches
• Energy-absorbing padded instrument panel and front seat-back tops • Thick laminate windshield • Safety armrests
• Safety steering wheel.

ACCIDENT PREVENTION FEATURES
• Side marker lights and reflectors • Parking lamps that illuminate with headlamps
• Four-way hazard warning flasher • Back-up lights • Lane change feature in direction signal control • Windshield defrosters, washer and dual-speed wipers • Wide-view inside mirror (vinyl-edged, shatter-resistant glass and deflecting support)
• Outside rearview mirror • Dual master cylinder brake system with warning light
• Starter safety switch.

ANTI-THEFT FEATURES • Anti-theft ignition key reminder buzzer • Anti-theft steering column lock • Anti-theft alarm system with concealed exterior switch, including (for the first time) the roof panels in its circuitry.

ENGINE AVAILABILITY

All states except California		Transmissions/Rear Axle Ratios			
				Automatic Transmission	
Engines	Power Rating†	4-Speed Manual	4-Speed Close-Ratio Manual	Below 4,000 Ft.	4,000 Ft. and Above
350 Cu. In. V8 (Std.)	185/175▲	3.36	NA	3.08	3.55
350 Cu. In. V8 (Avail. RPO L82)●	220	3.70/3.36*	3.70	3.55	NA
California only					
350 Cu. In. V8	175	NA	NA	3.55	NA

†S.A.E. net horsepower as installed. *Available highway ratio. ▲Rating with High Altitude Emission Equipment.
STD.—Standard. NA—Not available.
●Not available California, Maryland, Florida, Oregon, Washington, also Boston, Chicago, Des Plaines (Ill.), Barrington (Ill.), Grand Rapids (Mi.) and Cook County (Ill.).
SPECIAL NOTE: California Emission Equipment required for registration in California. In other states, High Altitude Emission Equipment may be required in areas 4,000 feet or more above sea level.

The 25th Anniversary Corvette.
   It stands alone today as it has since the summer of 1953, a truly unique and finely machined two-seater, America's only true production sports car.
   The legend lives on and improves, as legends do, with the passage of time.

The Silver Anniversary Corvette: Twenty-five years in the making, we've enjoyed every minute of it.
   And now, if you will, a round of applause for the Corvette founding Harley Earl, Zora Arkus-Duntov, Bill Mitchell, Ed Cole...

Available on any Corvette are many Options and Custom Features. Many are illustrated or described in this catalog. Availability often depends on the model and other equipment selected. Your Ch

o for the countless men and women who've had a hand in building and
Corvettes over the years. For everyone who has ever owned
ette, driven one, loved one. Or dreamed about owning one someday.
ich, we'd imagine, includes just about everybody.

The folding brochure (pages 60-61) could be unfolded into a
poster, and included on its back this lady in triplicate with her
silver 1978 model dream car. Below is the title page of a 1979
folding brochure that also included a surprise—a drawn poster.
(see page 64).

Corvette

1979

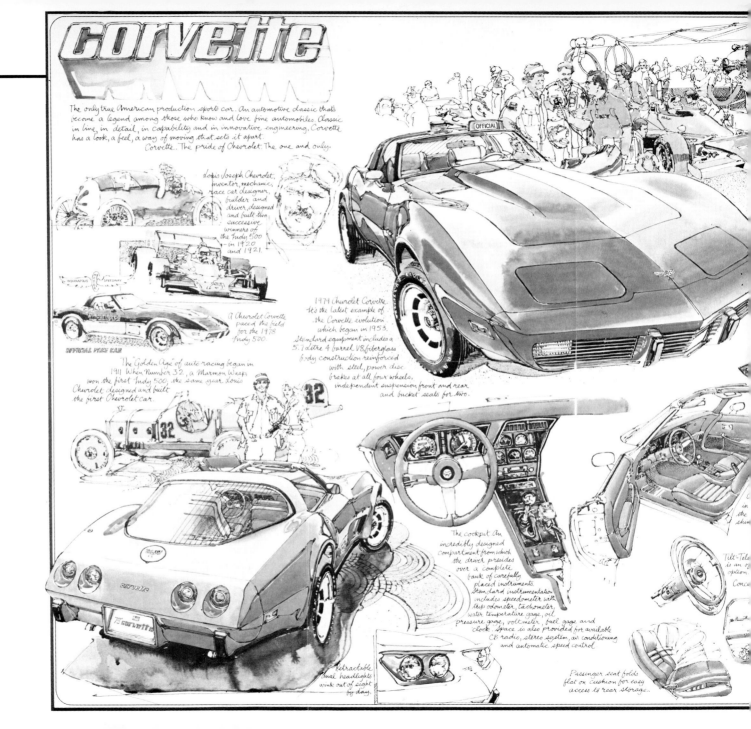

Corvette

The only true American production sports car. An automotive classic that's become a legend among those who know and love fine automobiles. Classic in line, in detail, in capability and in innovative engineering, Corvette has a look, a feel, a way of moving that sets it apart.

Corvette... The pride of Chevrolet. The one and only.

Louis Joseph Chevrolet, inventor, mechanic, race car designer, builder and driver, designed and built two successive winners of the Indy 500 — in 1920 and 1921.

A Chevrolet Corvette paced the field for the 1978 Indy 500.

OFFICIAL PACE CAR

The "Golden Age" of auto racing began in 1911 when Number 32, a Marmon Wasp, won the first Indy 500, the same year Louis Chevrolet designed and built the first Chevrolet car.

1979 Chevrolet Corvette. It's the latest example of the Corvette evolution which began in 1953. Standard equipment includes a 5.7 litre 4 barrel V8, fiberglass body construction reinforced with steel, power disc brakes at all four wheels, independent suspension front and rear and bucket seats for two.

The cockpit. An incredibly designed compartment from which the driver presides over a complete bank of carefully placed instruments. Standard instrumentation includes speedometer with trip odometer, tachometer, water temperature gage, oil pressure gage, voltmeter, fuel gage and clock. Space is also provided for available CB radio, stereo system, air conditioning and automatic speed control.

Retractable dual headlights wink out of sight by day.

Tilt-Tele... is an option. Conce...

Passenger seat folds flat on cushion for easy access to rear storage.

Build your own Corvette.

(See your dealer for current ordering information and specific model/option availability.)

COLORS

Exterior color _____
Interior color† _____
Upholstery _____

ENGINES
(See Power Teams chart for details on engine and transmission availability.)
☐ 5.7 Litre 4-Bbl. V8 (350 Cu. In.) (Std.)
☐ 5.7 Litre 4-Bbl. V8 (350 Cu. In.) L82 (Avail.)*

TRANSMISSIONS
☐ Four-Speed manual*
☐ Four-Speed manual close-ratio*
☐ Automatic

AVAILABLE OPTIONS
☐ Air conditioning.
☐ Removable tinted glass roof panels.
☐ Tilt-Telescopic steering wheel.

*Not available in California or with High Altitude Emission Equipment.

☐ Automatic speed control.
☐ Electric rear window defogger.
☐ Power windows.
☐ Power windows and door locks.
☐ Sport mirrors, LH remote and RH manual.
☐ Convenience Group (includes time-delay dome and courtesy lights, headlight warning buzzer, underhood light, low fuel warning light, color-keyed floor mats, intermittent windshield wipers and RH visor vanity mirror).

SOUND EQUIPMENT
☐ AM/FM stereo/Citizens Band radio with tri-band power antenna.
☐ AM/FM stereo radio.
☐ AM/FM stereo radio with 8-track stereo tape.

☐ AM/FM stereo radio with stereo cassette tape.
☐ Power antenna.
☐ Dual rear speakers.

TIRES
☐ P225/70R-15 steel-belted radial ply white-lettered tires.
☐ P255/60R-15 aramid-belted radial ply white-lettered tires.

MISCELLANEOUS
☐ Aluminum wheels.
☐ Gymkhana suspension.
☐ Chassis equipment — trailering.
☐ Heavy-duty battery.
☐ Highway axle ratio.
☐ Heavy-duty shock absorbers.

† Leather or cloth and leather interior colors available: light beige, dark blue, dark green, oyster. Leather only: black, red.

A word about assembly, components and optional equipment in these Chevrolets.

The Chevrolets described in this brochure are assembled at facilities of General Motors Corporation operated by the GM Assembly Division. These vehicles incorporate thousands of different components produced by various divisions of General Motors and by various suppliers to General Motors. From time to time during the manufacturing process, it may be necessary, in order to meet public demand for particular vehicles or equipment, or to meet federally mandated emissions, safety and fuel economy requirements, or for other reasons, to produce Chevrolet products with different components or differently sourced components than initially scheduled. All such components have been approved for use in Chevrolet products and will provide the quality performance associated with the Chevrolet name.

With respect to extra cost optional equipment, make certain you specify the type of equipment you desire on your vehicle when ordering it from your dealer. Some options may be unavailable when your car is built. Your dealer receives advice regarding current availability of options. You may ask the dealer for this information. GM also requests the dealer to advise you if an option you ordered is unavailable. We suggest you verify that your car includes the optional equipment you ordered or, if there are changes, that they are acceptable to you.

The combination of various extras to make a "personal" car inspired the GMC writers to say: Build yourself your own Corvette!

In line with the Corvette philosophy of evolutionary development is a brand-new assembly plant in Bowling Green, Kentucky, that will replace during this year the plant at St. Louis, where Corvettes have been built for 28 years. The Bowling Green facility, which will build Corvettes exclusively, is an investment in Corvette's future. It represents the experience and knowledge learned over all those years, which are reflected in the state-of-the-art innovative technology used to build Corvettes.

Just one of these modern technological innovations is a new paint process. In addition to many solid colors, four new optional two-tone treatments celebrate the opening of the new plant. All solid and two-tone metallics employ a base coat/clear coat application for outstanding beauty. This method allows use of glamor metallics with large-flake high-metallic content. And the clear acrylic enamel finish

coat gives a depth of luster not possible with conventional paint finishes. It also provides a measure of protection against the elements.

The four two-tone color combinations are shown on this page. See the back cover for solid color listing.

Dark E

Silver Metallic
over Charcoal Metallic

"What you see here is constant striving to build road machine. The plant and are two examples of Chevrolet's com

Claret Metallic
over Dark Claret Metallic

Silver Metallic
over Dark Blue Metallic

**Pages from a 1981
Corvette brochure.**

Corvette is a rolling showcase of new technology, new materials and new thinking—all part of an evolutionary process that continues year after year. Adherence to the principle of engineering excellence has been applied to all areas, from the front bumpers to the aircraft-style cockpit to the rear suspension system. It is these kinds of developments—detailed here—that make Corvette what it is today: one of the most renowned two-seat sports cars in the world.

For 1981, Corvette engineers trod where none have gone before by developing the world's first and only fiberglass-reinforced composite automotive spring (used with automatic transmission only). It even won the Society of Plastic Engineers Grand Award. This monoleaf rear spring—at 8 lbs.—replaces a 41-lb. steel multileaf spring. And it's not just lighter, it's more efficient. It can store six times the strain-energy per unit weight than a comparable weight of spring steel. This is the lightest possible leaf spring application to be found in any automotive suspension. And steel interleaf friction is eliminated. This fiberglass spring supports the weight of the car that rests on the rear wheels and provides suspension compliance. Wheel position is controlled by a system of links and pivots.

Attention to detail for 1981 includes other engineering developments such as magnesium valve rocker covers and stainless steel exhaust manifolds. And an

Aluminum Axle Assembly

Fiberglass Spring

"We critique Corvette with the same engineering objectivity we'd use to evaluate a military aircraft: What is Corvette's mission? How well does it carry out that mission?"

Dave McLellan,
Chief Engineer, Corvette

our
stem
quality."
Dave McLellan

1982 CORVETTE

Chevy makes good things happen.

Corvette Coupe.

Chevrolet

1982 Corvette
This is a whole new kind of Corvette.

It is still the road-rapacious sports car that's always been capable of inhaling great chunks of tormented 2-lane tarmac and leaving you exhilarated even after long, 1000-mile days in the saddle. It's still the time and space machine it's always been.

But there's a new civility now, predicated in large part on two engineering advances for 1982. Cross-fire fuel injection and a 4-speed automatic transmission with overdrive fourth gear so good in every aspect of driving usage that the manual transmission has been deleted.

There's a new quality about Corvette too. A space age standard of fit and finish quality that is rigidly imposed and then double-checked by workers and inspectors at Corvette's new 1-million-square-foot plant in Bowling Green, Kentucky.

And for this year, a unique and distinguished Corvette...the special "Collector Edition".

This is the Corvette to covet. From its raised white-lettered Eagle GT tires to its frameless hatchback, the "Collector Edition" is, we believe, the finest all-around 2-seater in the world.

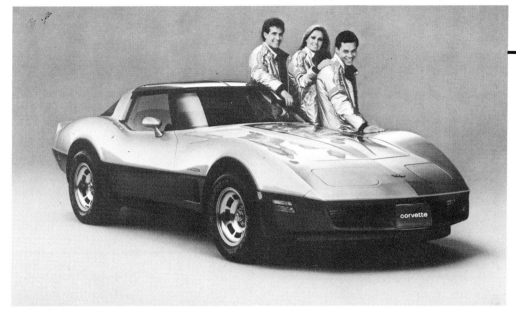

Corvette Coupe.

Frameless glass-hatch design with remote release is standard on the "Collector Edition" Hatchback Coupe.

Aircraft-style centre console and full gauge instrumentation are standard. NOTE: Speedometers in Canada have major scale in km/h, secondary in mph and odometer in kilometres.

Corvette standard interior.

**Simple in printing and layout is this brochure.
But it shows all the details.**

Corvette Major Standard Equipment

EXTERIOR	Corvette Sport Coupe	Corvette Collector Edition
Anti-theft alarm system with starter-interrupt feature	S	S
Front fender louvres	S	S
Front cornering lamps	S	S
Specific "Collector Edition" emblems – front, sides, rear	NA	S
Power-operated retractable headlamps	S	S
Quad headlamps with halogen hi-beam inner units	S	S
Dual remote-controlled outside sport mirrors	S	S
Tinted glass	S	S
Special silver-beige metallic finish	NA	S
Removable roof panels with solar screening	EC	S
Steel wheels with centre hub and trim rings	S	NA
Finned aluminum wheels	NA	S
Frameless rear hatch glass with remote release	NA	S
Body-colour front bumper with integral air dam	S	S
Energy-absorbing bumper systems	S	S
Corrosion-resistant steel-reinforced fiberglass body	S	S
Concealed dual-speed wipers with integral washers and wiper arms	S	S
INTERIOR		
Leather-trimmed vinyl or all-cloth bucket seats	S	NA
Full-leather bucket seats	NA	S
Soft-padded and carpeted door panels	S	S
Moulded shell seats with high-pivot folding backs	S	S
Power windows	S	S
Electric rear window defroster	S	S
AM/FM push-button radio with dual front speakers and mast antenna	S	S
Air conditioning	S	S
Time-delay dome and courtesy lights	S	S
Headlamp-on reminder	S	S
Low-fuel warning lamp	S	S
Illuminated RH visor vanity mirror	S	S
Leather-wrapped steering wheel rim	S	S
Tilt-Telescopic steering wheel and column	S	S
Glove compartment lock and lamp	S	S
Intermittent windshield wipers	S	S
7,000-RPM electronic tachometer	S	S
Voltmeter, temperature, fuel and oil pressure gauges	S	S
Quartz analog electric clock with sweep-second hand	S	S

	Corvette Sport Coupe	Corvette Collector Edition
Cigarette lighter and ashtray	S	S
Resettable trip odometer	S	S
Centre console with shifter, coin tray, window, mirror and air conditioning controls	S	S
Day/night rearview mirror	S	S
Deep-twist floor and stowage area carpet	S	S
Acoustical insulation package	S	S
Luggage compartment concealment shade	S	S
POWER TEAMS/CHASSIS/MECHANICAL		
Computer Command Control	S	S
5.7 Litre CFI V8 engine (Cross-Fire Injection)	S	S
Automatic transmission with overdrive fourth gear	S	S
Aluminum intake manifold with tuned runners	S	S
Stainless steel exhaust manifolds and free-flow mufflers	S	S
Hydraulic valve lifters and exhaust valve rotators	S	S
Magnesium valve rocker covers	S	S
Black wrinkle-finish air cleaner	S	S
Hood outside-air duct	S	S
Electric in-tank fuel pump	S	S
Low-drag engine primary cooling fan	S	S
Auxiliary electric engine cooling fan	S	S
High Energy Ignition system	S	S
Freedom II battery with sealed side terminals	S	S
Power steering with ball-race gear	S	S
Power disc brakes at all four wheels	S	S
Exclusive monoleaf fiberglass rear spring design	S	S
New driveshaft seals and splash shields	S	S
New, larger drive shaft universal joints	S	S
Sturdy frame structure with corrosion-resistant coating	S	S
Fully independent four-wheel suspension	S	S
Delcotron generator with built-in solid-state regulator	S	S
P225/70R-15B steel-belted radial ply tires	S	NA
P225/60R-15B steel-belted radial ply white-lettered tires	EC	S
Compact spare tire	S	S
Side-lift jack	S	S
Underhood lamp	S	S

S–Standard   EC–Optional at Extra Cost   NA–Not Available

Options

Listed below are some of the available equipment choices to help you customize your 1982 Corvette. For other optional equipment and their availability, see your Chevrolet dealer.

• Electric twin remote control sport mirrors • Roof panel carrier • Power door lock system • Delco radios: AM/FM stereo radio • Electronically tuned stereo radio with 8-track tape player • Electronically tuned stereo radio with cassette tape player • Electronically tuned stereo radio with Citizens Band and cassette tape • Power antenna (included with Citizens Band radio) • Removable glass roof panels • Automatic speed control with 'resume speed' feature • Gymkhana suspension includes rear stabilizer and bushings, higher-rate springs and special shock absorbers • Tires: P225/70R-15 or P225/60R-15 steel-belted radial ply white-lettered • Six-way power driver's seat • Aluminum wheels • Custom two-tone exterior paint.

Exterior Colours

Choose from 11 high-lustre acrylic finishes or several available Two-Tone combinations. Colours: White, Silver Metallic, Black, Silver Blue Metallic, Dark Blue Metallic, Silver Green Metallic, Bright Blue Metallic, Gold Metallic, Charcoal Metallic, Red, Dark Claret Metallic.

Corvette "Collector Edition" features an exclusive Silver Beige Metallic exterior finish.

Interiors

Corvette is available in a choice of four cloth interiors: Silver Gray, Dark Blue, Camel and Dark Red; or select from six available leather trims: Silver Gray, Charcoal, Dark Blue, Green, Camel or Dark Red.

Corvette "Collector Edition": features full leather seats in an exclusive Silver Beige multi-tone trim.

Safety Features

OCCUPANT PROTECTION

Manual lap/shoulder belts with push-button buckles for driver and right front passenger (driver's side includes visual and audible warning system) • Energy-absorbing steering column • Passenger guard door locks • Safety door latches and stamped steel hinges • Folding seat back latches • Energy-absorbing padded instrument panel with anti-reflective upper surface • Laminated windshield/tempered side and rear glass • Safety armrests • Identification symbols for controls and displays.

ACCIDENT AVOIDANCE

Side marker lights and reflectors • Parking lamps that illuminate with headlamps • Four-way hazard warning flasher • Backup lights • Lane change feature in direction signal control • Windshield defrosters, washer and dual-speed wipers with time-delay feature • Vinyl-edged inside mirror • Dual outside rearview mirrors • Dual master cylinder brake system with warning light • Starter safety switch.

ANTI-THEFT

Audible anti-theft ignition key reminder • Anti-theft steering column lock • Anti-theft audio alarm system with starter-interrupt feature • Inside hood release.

A word about assembly, components and optional equipment in these vehicles.

The vehicles described in this brochure are assembled at various Divisions of General Motors Corporation. These vehicles incorporate thousands of different components produced by General Motors of Canada Limited and related companies and their suppliers. From time to time during the manufacturing process, it may be necessary, in order to meet public demand for particular vehicles or equipment, or to meet federally mandated emission and safety requirements or fuel economy guidelines, or for other reasons, to produce vehicles with different components or differently sourced components than initially scheduled. All such components have been approved for use in our products by General Motors of Canada Limited or related companies and will provide the quality performance associated with our name.

Please note that certain optional equipment can be ordered only in conjunction with other optional equipment. Also, upgrading from specified standard equipment may be necessary when certain optional equipment is ordered. Ask your sales representative for details.

With respect to extra cost optional equipment, make certain you specify the type of equipment you desire on your vehicle when ordering it from your dealer. Some options may be unavailable when your car is built. Your dealer receives advice regarding current availability of options. You may ask the dealer for this information. GM also requests the dealer to advise you if an option you ordered is unavailable. We suggest you verify that your car includes the optional equipment you ordered or, if there are changes, that they are acceptable to you.

All illustrations and specifications contained in this catalogue are based on the latest product information available at time of publication approval. The right is reserved to make changes at any time, without notice, in prices, colours, materials, equipment, specifications and models, and to discontinue models. Some of the equipment shown or described throughout this catalogue is available at extra cost. Check with your Chevrolet dealer for complete information.

General Motors of Canada Limited
Oshawa, Ontario

Printed in Canada

November 1981

Technical details of the 1982 model Corvette. Plenty of information on the "Collector Edition".

Multi-tone full leather seats highlight the "Collector Edition" special interior.

Corvette Collector Edition Hatchback Coupe.

Exterior Dimensions: Millimetres (Inches)

Wheelbase	2489 (98.0)
Length (overall)	4707 (185.3)
Width (overall)	1753 (69.0)
Height (loaded)	1219 (48.0)
Tread – front	1491 (58.7)
Tread – rear	1511 (59.5)
Fuel tank capacity: Litres (gals)	90.8 (20)

Interior Dimensions: Millimetres (Inches)

Head room – front	919 (36.2)
Leg room – front	1069 (42.1)
Hip room – front	1267 (49.9)
Shoulder room – front	1206 (47.5)
Usable trunk capacity: Litres (cu. ft.)	234 (8.4)

Corvette Power Teams

Engine	Ordering Code	Displacement (cu. in.)	Engine Availability	Transmission Availability
5.7 Litre Cross-fire Injection V8(A)	L83	350	Std.	Std. 4-speed automatic with overdrive

Std. = Standard   (A) = Produced by GM – Chevrolet Motor Division, U.S.A.
Computer Command Control System (NB1) standard.
Caution: The use of leaded fuel will cause the Computer Command Control System to malfunction.

See your Chevrolet salesperson for Transport Canada approved fuel consumption estimates for all Corvette models.

A WORD ABOUT ENGINES
Some Chevrolets are equipped with engines produced by other GM division, subsidiaries, or affiliated companies worldwide. See your dealer for details.

Export-oriented: data in metrics! The motor's performance has decreased drastically . . .

COMMITMENT

The fact that the first chapter in this Corvette brochure concerns the final chapter in the Corvette building process is in itself significant. We are committed to excellence in the production of the product, in

The Corvette plant, Bowling Green, Kentucky.

order to achieve excellence in the product.

A good example of the totality of the Corvette commitment is the scene pictured here—"The Morning Audit." Each morning, salaried

and hourly employe examine cars in deta search for ways to a enhance the quality o

It is typical of the a detail in evidence th the new Corvette pla

10

A new generation: Corvette catalog for the 1983 model year.

Green. One plant, one
group of people,
dedicated to building one
fine model, at a
sedate pace of just a few
an hour.

11

The Corvette appeared in completely new form for the 1983 model year. Only the V8 fuel—injection powerplant with its 350 SAE HP remained. This Corvette had lost much of its original "bite", but meanwhile a new automobile generation had grown up, applying completely different yardsticks...

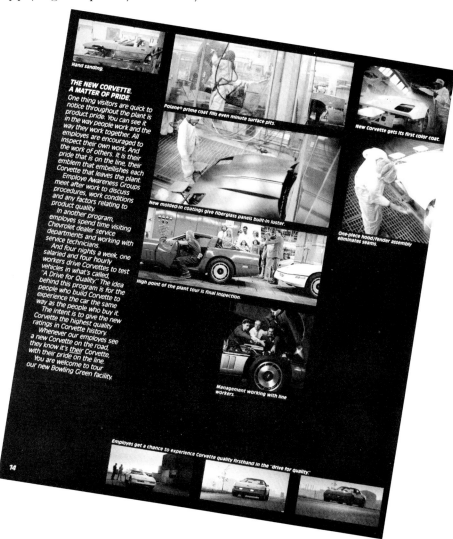

Hand sanding.

THE NEW CORVETTE. A MATTER OF PRIDE.
One thing visitors are quick to notice throughout the plant is product pride. You can see it in the way people work and the way they work together. All employes are encouraged to inspect their own work. And the work of others. It is their pride that is on the line, their emblem that embellishes each Corvette that leaves the plant.
Employe Awareness Groups meet after work to discuss procedures, work conditions and any factors relating to product quality.
In another program, employes spend time visiting Chevrolet dealer service departments and working with service technicians.
And four nights a week, one salaried and four hourly workers drive Corvettes to test vehicles in what's called, "A Drive for Quality." The idea behind this program is for the people who build Corvette to experience the car the same way as the people who buy it. The intent is to give the new Corvette the highest quality ratings in Corvette history.
Whenever our employes see a new Corvette on the road, they know it's their Corvette, with their pride on the line. You are welcome to tour our new Bowling Green facility.

Polane® prime coat fills even minute surface pits.

New Corvette gets its first color coat.

New molded-in coatings give fiberglass panels built-in luster.

One-piece hood/fender assembly eliminates seams.

High point of the plant tour is final inspection.

Management working with line workers.

Employes get a chance to experience Corvette quality firsthand in the "drive for quality".

14

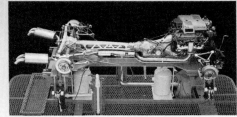

You'd expect the new Corvette to brake handily and it does. With a Girlock four-wheel disc brake system, the new Corvette can decelerate from its top speed as high as 1.0g. Girlock is internationally respected for high performance and racing brake expertise. The low-drag, aluminum caliper design for the new Corvette effects a considerable weight savings over previous Corvette four-wheel disc systems, which helps to reduce unsprung mass. The resulting vehicle dynamics are impressive.

With the standard suspension and the optional Goodyear Eagle VR tires, lateral acceleration is rated at 0.9g on our skidpad, in the hands of a professional driver.

1.0g is equal to the pull of gravity. Cornering or braking at 1.0g means we are encountering a horizontal component (or force) equal in pull to the gravity vector (or the full weight of the car). With Corvette's 0.9g reading, the lateral force is equal to 90% of the weight of the car.

There is an optional suspension, the Z51 Performance Handling Package. It generates 0.95g under lateral accelera-tion on GM's skidpad. Readings in this range are remarkable, yet Corvette is still a able car to drive.

The Z51 incorpora 9½" rear wheels, lar stabilizer bars, 25mr 23mm rear. Different are used, allowing low while cornering. The

36

The impression is aggressive again—even if from unusual photo angles—but also thoroughly detailed.

of the proven and efficient
racing engineering practices.
The use of forged aluminum
suspension components
reduced unsprung mass by
nearly 30%, which contributes
to wheel control, ride and road
holding. The payoff is that the
new Corvette has demonstrated
remarkable directional stability
and transient response in
surface testing on the GM
proving grounds.
　The new Corvette. A true
world-class sports car.

s, too, in the stiffness
rglass monoleaf
both front and rear
valving of the shocks.
ratio, power-assisted
inion steering of
ckage makes for
onse to driver control

pension of the new
a totally integrated
which reflects many

**Meanwhile the Targa roll bar
has become a styling element.**

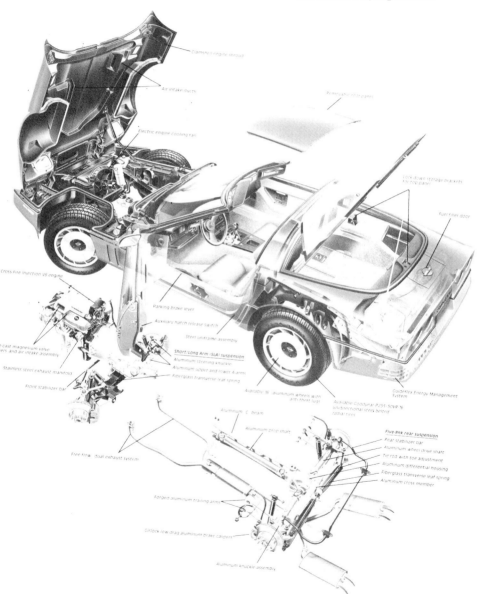

Clamshell engine shroud

Air intake ducts

Electric engine cooling fan

Cross-fire injection V8 engine

Parking brake lever

Auxiliary hatch release switch

Steel uniframe assembly

Short/Long Arm (SLA) suspension
Aluminum steering knuckle
Aluminum upper and lower A-arms
Fiberglass transverse leaf spring

Die cast magnesium valve
covers, and air intake assembly

Stainless steel exhaust manifold

Front stabilizer bar

Removable roof panel

Lock-down storage brackets
for top panel

Fuel filler door

Available 16" aluminum wheels with
anti-theft lugs

Guideflex Energy Management
System

Available Goodyear P255-50VR 16
unidirectional steel-belted
radial tires

Aluminum "C" beam

Aluminum prop shaft

Five-link rear suspension
Rear stabilizer bar
Aluminum wheel drive shaft
Tie rod with toe adjustment
Aluminum differential housing
Fiberglass transverse leaf spring
Aluminum cross member

Free-flow dual exhaust system

Forged aluminum trailing arms

Girlock low drag aluminum brake calipers

Aluminum knuckle assembly

CORVETTE

Catalog
of the
1986
model.

76

The most beautiful
Corvette catalog
ever—with 44 pages
and additional
sheets of data. The
photos are also of
excellent quality.

NEEDLES, SOUTH DAKOTA. NAMED FOR THE SHARP PEAKS THAT JUT UP FROM THE GRASSES OF THE GREAT PLAINS. HOME OF PRAIRIE DOGS AND BISON, HOST BRIEFLY TO CORVETTE.

AMERICA THE VAST WHERE ROADS THAT STRETCH STRAIGHT TO THE HORIZON ARE AN IDEAL AND INVITING PROVING GROUND FOR THE POWER THAT PULSES THROUGH CORVETTE.

You'd think the sky is the sky everywhere. But people who've grown up under unbroken western vistas feel hemmed in when they travel eastward. And those who like their sky in bits and pieces gaze 360°, shiver a little and say, "There's too much sky," when they go out West.

In the Corvette Convertible you do more than travel under the sky. You become part of it. With nothing between you and the changing face of America...the pungence of freshly turned farmland...the wind blowing from Idaho to Indiana...the Rockies thrust up along the spine of the continent ...deserts spread over endless arid miles.

Before long the car assumes the aura of its occupant. Temperature and airflow set to particular preferences. Favorite traveling music modulated precisely. A sweater tossed aside.

When you climb aboard after a brief rest stop, you simply assume everything will be as you left it. After all, you and the Corvette form a private world.

Private but never anonymous. Not in this car. From urban streetside to rural truck stop to western national park, the roadster draws a crowd. Murmurs of approval follow. Children dash excitedly from nose to spoiler as young couples grip hands and promise each other, "Someday." Everybody recognizes the Convertible. Most want to touch it as if a piece of The Dream might rub off. And as the machine speeds into the distance, admiration for its beauty mixes with the wish to be going anywhere in the envious glances of those left behind.

Maybe that's because America and cars

GOODYEAR VR50 TIRES
The standard tire and wheel combination features P255/50VR 16 Goodyear unidirectional steel-belted radial tires mounted on 16" aluminum alloy wheels with functional turbine-blade design and anti-theft nuts.

ROOF PANEL STORAGE (COUPE)
The removable one-piece roof panel combines the security of a closed car with the exhilarating effects of an open roadster. There is no T-bar. The roof is removed using a ratchet wrench designed for this application. The panel may then be stored within the car in a lockdown position.

HALOGEN FOG LAMPS
The integral halogen fog lamps make driving under adverse conditions easier. Operation is independent of the headlamps.

CLOTH BUCKET SEATS
The high-back cloth bucket seats are contoured to provide the feeling of individualized fit and comfort. Manual back angle adjustment is offered. Other interior features include a leather-wrapped steering wheel, dual rear lockable storage compartments* lighted visor vanity mirror.

TILT-TELESCOPIC STEERING WHEEL
Corvette adjusts to your driving style with a steering wheel that tilts and telescopes.

4-SPEED AUTOMATIC TRANSMISSION
Four-speed automatic overdrive transmission with lockup torque converter contributes to impressive performance plus low-RPM highway cruising.

4-SPEED MANUAL TRANSMISSION
If you prefer, choose the smooth-shifting manual 4-speed, with an electronic automatic overdrive feature in 2nd, 3rd and 4th gear, which is available at no extra cost. Gear ratios are chosen to deliver exceptional performance.

CORVETTE NEWS
A three-year complimentary subscription goes to every Corvette buyer. This publication keeps owners up to date on their favorite sports car.

*Coupe only.

CORVETTE'S AIR CONDITIONING ALLOWS YOU TO MAINTAIN A PERFECT DRIVING ENVIRONMENT

RETRACTABLE HEADLAMPS FLIP FORWARD 162.5 DEGREES FROM BENEATH THE HOOD

VATS EMPLOYS A DECODER AND IGNITION KEY WITH A PELLET OF SPECIFIED RESISTANCE.

GOODYEAR EAGLE GT P255/50VR 16 UNIDIRECTIONAL RADIAL TIRES.

THE REMOVABLE ONE-PIECE ROOF LIFT-OFF PANEL STORES IN A LOCKDOWN POSITION IN THE REAR COMPARTMENT OPENING CORVETTE UP TO SUN AND STARS.

Motor sport: certainly not a dominant Corvette theme—but very photogenic . . .

The heart of the '86 Corvette—the
5.74 liter V8 motor with power
decreased to 208 HP. Fuel injection
has meanwhile become taken for
granted.

CORVETTE, A GENERATION:
25 YEARS OF MEN, MACHINES, AND MEMORIES.

1953-1955

January 1953: Harley Earl presents the Corvette at the New York Motorama show. In May of 1953 the car is ready for series production, four weeks later the first car of a 300-piece series appears. In September of 1954 a V8 motor is also available. The roadster acquires cranked windows and a hardtop in the autumn of 1955.

1956-1957

In September of 1956 the Corvette is equipped with fuel injection. For the 1958 model year the car gets double headlights and more chrome.

Corvette — Auto einer Generation

1958-1960

GM Designer Bill Mitchell works on a model with new bodywork; it later becomes famous as the Sting Ray. In the summer of 1960 the 10,000th Corvette of the current model series is built. The 1961 car with a new tail is presented.

1961-1962

In February of 1961 the Sting Ray makes its debut in Chicago as a show car. In December of 1962 disc brakes and more powerful V8 motors are tested.

1963-1967

As of the end of 1963 the rear window of the coupe no longer has a notch. One year later the Corvette gains disc brakes all around. 6.5, and 7-liter motors are offered. The 1966 model is "stylistically reworked"; the motors no longer have fuel injection. In April of 1967 a high-performance version (L88) comes out, with 435 HP (and no heating system).

1968-1977

Very reworked body and interior design, similar to the "Mako Shark II" show car. In November of 1969 the 250,000th Corvette leaves the factory in St. Louis. In February of 1970 GM produces a new 7.5-liter motor—with up to 460 HP. Body changes in the fall of 1973. Great festivities at General Motors: in March of 1977 the 500,000th Corvette is built.

(from a spring 1978 brochure)

83

Books for the Corvette Fan

Chevrolet—A History from 1911—by Beverly Rae Kimes and Robert Ackerson. In this history book the Corvette finds its rightful place; above all, the color photos are excellent. The book includes 200 pages and 160 photos, most in color.

Corvette, an American Legend—by Automobile Quarterly. One of the most exhaustive and best-made books on the subject of the Corvette. Cars of the 1953 to 1967 model years, absolutely authentic and part of a certain competition (Bloomington), are stressed particularly. 184 pages, 200 very good color pictures. English text.

Corvette—by B. Coleman. A collection of Corvette history in 100 pages (1953-1983) with 100 photos, most in color. A good overview (English text) for quick information.

Classic Corvettes in a Nutshell—by John F. Ball. Buying advice from an expert, full of useful tips (English text). 102 pages, 22 illustrations.

Corvette 1953-1967m A Source Book—by Arthur A. C. Steffen. A 144-page facsimile edition of old sales literature and advertisements, also dealer information from General Motors. An interesting source of authentic basic information "from that time", with over 300 illustrations.

Corvette—the Legend lives on. The continuation of the Bloomington theme for cars of the 1968 to 1982 model years, by Automobile Quarterly (see above). 200 pages, 250 color photos.

Early Chevrolet Corvettes—by C. Falconer. A volume in the Auto History Series (English text). All six- and eight-cylinder 1953-1967 models are described here. 136 pages, 60 b/w photos, 8 color pages.

Corvette Performance—everything about the development of this car as a sports and racing car (English text). Racing and test reports, club information. 458 illustrations on 180 pages.

Corvette, Amerikas Sportwagen—by Jay Koblenz. A 256 page German-language book from Serag Publishing, with the whole history of the American two-seater. 250 b/w and 145 color photos. A readable and well-made book for the enthusiast.

The Complete Book of the Corvette—by Richard M. Langworth. The prominent American automobile historian wrote this outstanding book, which presents all models through 1987. 320 pages, over 400 photos, most in color.

Corvette 1953-1980 Identification and Number Codes. All chassis numbers and motor data, gear specifications and so on for the 1953 to 1980 model years, also paint colors (from 1963 on) and extras. For the Corvette owner—who wants to know absolutely precisely—this is a valuable reference book.

Corvette Restoration Handbook. A restoration guide for the amateur, very well done, with more that 300 illustrations (English text) on 248 pages. All models to 1967 are included.

Corvette Sting Ray—by Robert Ackerson. A Super-Profile volume with exhaustive type histories, restoration tips and bibliography. 56 pages, 20 color photos.

Corvette, Sports Car for America—by M. B. Antonick. A well-made retrospective of the developmental history of the Corvette from 1953 to 1955, with contemporary advertising material and other illustrations. 240 pages, 200 b/w and 55 color photos. English text. The author has also written another book on the Corvette, covering only special competition cars.

The Complete Corvette Restoration and Technical Guide— by N. Adams. An expensive but indispensible book for the restorer. With 1400 illustrations on 424 pages. As thorough and informative as it can be! English text.

The Road Corvette—by R. Miller and G. Embree. Over 100 photos of all models and derivatives from 1953 to 1973 are in this book, which ranks among the classics of Corvette literature. It has 320 pages and includes, among other things, complete technical data in detail.

Corvette Body Repair Guide—by Robert J. Schiro. For the repair of plastic bodies this is a valuable helper. All processes are shown in pictures (250 illustrations, also in color). The book is spiral-bound and includes 200 pages.

(There are also various other publications, all from American publishers, as well as buyers' guides and road test reprints. The automobile book mail-order houses and specialty shops offer an inclusive selection of Corvette literature.)

The Corvette in the Press

In August of 1953 the first reports on the new Corvette appeared in the American motoring press. They scarcely went beyond a description of the model—road tests were not published before the spring of 1954. A first impression in *Road & Track* read as follows:

"Ever since 1948 we have raised the question again and again of an American sports car. Now we have it in the form of the Chevrolet Corvette. We learned, to be sure, during a test drive to Chicago and New York that this car is as yet scarcely known to sports-car enthusiasts—and many don't believe at all that this car is really a sports car!" Thus John R. Bond set out to convince his readers. He quoted the construction principles laid down by Maurice Olley and called the Corvette a "pleasant contrast to many pseudo-sports cars such as are offered under other General Motors brand names". Yet: there were a few question marks between the lines.

When the Corvette appeared with a V8 motor, the motoring press acted happier. But there was criticism of the gears and the brakes: "The enthusiast is not to be convinced of them. What is the point of the slogan—For Experts only—? It takes no particular talent to drive the Corvette . . ." What was wanted above all was a manual transmission. And that was finally at hand to be tested in the 1956 model. *Road & Track* wrote: "At first glance one thinks three gears are not enough. But the ratios are excellently chosen. 100 miles in second gear! This new Corvette promises to become a very interesting car for the enthusiast who wants a good all-around car. It might even have a chance in Class C for production cars (3 to 5 liters)

and there provide a certain liveliness . . ."

Journalists from *Sports Cars Illustrated* rated the 1956 Corvette as "good to excellent". They stressed the acceleration above all, measured at 7.4 seconds from a standing start to 100 kph. The top speed was measured at 130 mph ' 209 kph. To be sure, they also found some vibration at high speeds, which *Road & Track* also confirmed: "Shuddering which did not exist before appeared at more than 100 mph, and the motor, it seems, also became rather loud . . ."

Nr. 867	Chevrolet Corvette Sport-Cabriolet		
Ausrüstung	Türen: 2		
	Synchromesh-Getriebe		
	Scheibenwaschanlage		
	Heizung und Entfroster		
	Handbrems-Warnlicht		
	Uhr		
	Elektrisch betätigtes Verdeck		
	Abnehmbares Kunststoff-Hardtop		
Motor	Steuer-PS		23,62
	Brems-PS bei U/Min.		233/4800
	Anzahl Zylinder		8
	Zylinderinhalt cm³		4637
	Bohrung mm		98,42
	Hub mm		76,20
	Kompressionsverhältnis		9,5:1
	Verhältnis Brems-PS		
	zu Gewicht kg/PS		6,1
Getriebe	Synchromesh-		
	Getriebeuntersetzung	I:	2,2:1
		II:	1,66:1
		III:	1,31:1
		IV:	1:1
		R:	2,26:1
	Hinterachse		3,7:1
Abmessungen	Länge mm		4488
und Gewichte	Breite mm		1788
	Höhe mm		1320
	Leergewicht fahrbereit kg		1430
	Radstand mm		2591
	Spur vorn mm		1448
	Spur hinten mm		1499
	Spurkreisdurchmesser m		11,10
	Pneugrösse		7,3×15
	Benzintankinhalt l		62

The 1958 Corvette was again greeted with much euphoria. "Two four-throat carburetors or fuel injection at a compression ratio of 10.5 : 1! A tachometer up to 8000 rpm! A powerfully proportioned clutch and a self-locking differential! A choice of three-speed manual or four-speed automatic ransmission! Sporting drivers as well as lovers of comfort get all they paid for . . ."

The frequent stylistic changes, commonplace in the USA, never drew criticism. The cockpit, the press found, got better from year to year, but it was about

One of the few German-language brochures (for Switzerland) limited itself to the listing of technical data and the names of General Motors dealers.

time (1959) to give the Corvette seat belts "for hard driving"—they were not yet mandatory. Otherwise there were just two points to criticize: a certain tendency to oversteer and a too-slow response of the motor to pressure on the gas pedal, which led to unwanted pauses in acceleration during shifting.

Now and then the plastic body was also criticized, but one could attribute no faults to it. "It is faultlessly made, and the joints of the individual parts are perfect. One notes that Chevrolet gives a lot of care to the body." The seats drew much praise. "Very well-formed and comfortable. Even on long trips there is no weariness at the wheel. A day in the Corvette is not stressful!" (1961).

Chevrolet-Vertretungen in der Schweiz
Distributeurs Chevrolet en Suisse

Aadorf	Eugen Ruckstuhl, Garage, Tel. (052) 4 73 19
Aarau	F. Glaus & Co., Hohlgass-Garage, Tel. (064) 2 13 33
Baden	B. Leoni AG, Bruggerstrasse 50, Tel. (056) 2 38 38
Basel	Agence Américaine Automobiles S.A., Viaduktstr. 45 (Postfach 105), Tel. (061) 24 66 66
Bern	Bellevue-Garage AG, Kochergasse 1, Tel. (031) 3 77 77
Bern	Gebr. Bärtschi AG, Länggass-Garage, Tel. (031) 3 36 33
Bern	Spiegl & Waber GmbH, Nordring 8, Tel. (031) 9 44 44
Bern	Hans Lack, Ostring-Garage, Freudenbergerplatz Tel. (031) 4 49 11
Biel	Burkhalter & Brändli, Garage, Freiestrasse 7, Tel. (032) 2 25 24
Buchs/SG	A. Sulser, Garage, Tel. (085) 6 14 14
La Chaux-de-Fonds	Garage Guttmann S.A., 110, rue de la Serre, tél. (039) 3 46 81
Chur	L. Dosch, Grand-Garage, Tel. (081) 2 13 13
Fribourg	L. & M. Baudère, Garage de Pérolles, tél. (037) 2 38 88
Genève	Etabl. Fleury & Cie S.A., rue de la Mairie 35, tél. (022) 36 62 30
Glarus	F. Schielly-Ryffel, Central-Garage, Tel. (058) 5 18 34
Interlaken	E. Zimmermann, Bahnhof-Garage, Tel. (036) 2 13 15
Langenthal	M. & E. Würgler, Garage, Tel. (063) 2 20 77
Lausanne	Etabl. Ch. Ramuz S.A., avenue d'Echallens 2a, tél. (021) 24 04 44
Liestal	Blank AG, Tiergartenweg 1, Tel. (061) 84 31 11
Lugano	Eredi di N. Crescionini, Via Stefano Franscini 8, tel. (091) 2 83 43
Luzern	Auto-Koch AG, Löwenplatz, Tel. (041) 2 77 77
Münsingen	Ernst Marti, Garage, Tel. (031) 68 15 15
Neuchâtel	Garage Schenker, Faubourg du Lac 29, tél. (038) 5 28 64
Porrentruy	Périat & Pétignat, Garage des Ponts, tél (066) 6 12 06
Reiden	Turmgarage, Luzernerstrasse, Tel. (062) 9 35 44
Sarnen	Cl. Sidler, Garage, Brünigstrasse, Tel. (041) 85 18 88
Schaffhausen/Neuhausen	Georg Neck, Garage Enge, Tel. (053) 6 94 55
Schattdorf	A. Brand-Stadler, Autogarage, Tel. (044) 2 13 88
Sion	G. Revaz, Garage de l'Ouest, tél. (027) 2 22 62
Solothurn	E. Kupferschmid & O. Müller, Tel. (065) 2 14 42
St. Gallen	E. Wagner, Centralgarage AG, Tel. (071) 22 55 22
St. Maurice	Jean-Jacques Casanova, Garage, tél. (025) 3 63 90
St. Moritz	Gebr. Cattaneo, Kulm-Garage, Tel. (082) 3 33 33
Sursee	O. & R. Wyder, Automobile, Bahnhofstrasse, Tel. (045) 4 22 22
Thun	Paul Wenger, Oberland-Garage, Tel. (033) 2 30 29
Weinfelden	J. Ammann-Grünert, Central-Garage, Tel. (072) 5 13 33
Wetzikon	B. Krähenmann, Werkgarage, Usterstrasse 46, Tel. (051) 97 87 02
Wil	Fürstenland-Garage AG, Tel. (073) 6 04 80
Winterthur	Eulach-Garage AG, Technikumstrasse 67, Tel. (052) 2 23 33
Yverdon	W. Humberset, Garage des Remparts, tél. (024) 2 35 35
Zug	Jos. Iten, Autos, Tel. (042) 4 23 23
Zürich	AG Vertretung Agence Américaine, Dufourstrasse 23, Tel. (051) 32 72 73

When the Sting Ray made its bow, it was greeted with applause. Even the *New York Times* devoted specific praise to it: "Really successful! Within ten years America's only sports car has developed into a thoroughbred vehicle, equally splendidly suited for street and sport."

The balanced weight distribution and independent suspension were pointed out particularly. *Motor Trend* wrote: "A noteworthy difference. The distance behind European sports cars rear, "is closed!" *Road & Track*: "The new Sting Ray sticks They hastened to add that the closing headlights were no joke from the stylists in Detroit, but rather gave aerodynamic advantages.

"Soon the Corvette was available with motors up to 375 HP. "Although so powerfully motorized, the car is gentle as a lamb to drive," it was said in a 1964 *Road & Track* test. And so much power was easy to control when linked to a four-speed automatic transmission. The reputation that the Corvette could enjoy after ten years of existence had grown greatly and was equal to that of Porsche. And: "Finally they eliminated the division of the rear window—a big improvement of the view to the There is also room for luggage in the Sting Ray—but it has to be lifted over the seats, for the car has no trunk lid. It would be good if the rear window could be opened, as in an Aston Martin" (a wish that was later fulfilled in a special model). "We would also like to criticize the seating conditions: the driver's space is very narrow—compared to the generous overall dimensions of the car." Otherwise: highest praise for the quality of workmanship.

In August of 1965 a 425 HP car was displayed to the press. "One might wish that this Corvette would cause a sensation in sports-car racing . . . but unfortunately the car would be too heavy for that", wrote *Road & Track*". In fact, the Corvette was 400 kilograms heavier than the Cobra. "It is obviously not a matter of how many horsepower, but how many one can put on the ground and use . . . Many sports cars could use more spice, but the Corvette is certainly not one of them." In the Seventies the press did not have much new to say about "America's only sports car". They repeated the hopes and expectations in terms of sports-car racing, also in the European motoring press.

The famous racing Corvette that had been prepared by Zora Arkus-Duntov in 1957 enjoyed a brief spotlight in the German motoring press. *Auto, Motor & Sport* reported on this car ("the only car with which General Motors ever officially participated in auto racing") and wrote:

"Because time was short, Duntov stripped a Mercedes 300 SL coupe and copied the tubular frame. Rumors at that time said that the frame was copied from that of the Jaguar D-Type, but a photo taken at that time proves that it was based on a 300 SL frame. It consisted of triangular tubes of chrome-molybdenum steel. Stronger tubes were mounted forward and aft to hold the suspension."

The bodies—there was one of light metal and one of plastic-weighed 82 kilograms each—exactly as much as the tubular frame. "The Corvette SS is very much lighter and smaller than the production car . . . the gross weight was only 900 kilograms."

The first test drives, it was reported, were made by Fangio and Moss. John Fitch and Piero Taruffi

Report on the 250 Miles of Daytona in "sportauto", January 1976. The Corvette of the American John Greenwood had 725 HP under its hood.

drove the car in the Sebring race. But the Corvette SS did not reach the finish line— because of a series of small but eventually decisive problems. The car was later put in a museum—it was never raced again.

Privately entered Corvettes meanwhile appeared in many sports car races, in the USA and elsewhere— with varying success. A highly tuned Sting Ray with over 700 HP took part, for example, in the Daytona 250 and other races in 1976. Yörn Pugmeister reported on the Corvette monster in *Sport Auto:*

"The external form is still reminiscent of 'the' American sports car, but John Greenwood created his own Corvette. First of all, he cut most of the original car's chassis away and replaced it with a tubular frame; then he gave the car new front and rear brakes . . ." Greenwood installed an 8.2 liter motor with 725 HP. Greenwood took the checkered flag with an average speed of 188 kph—more than half a minute ahead of Brian Redman in a BMW 3.0 CSL.

The Corvette of the early Eighties likewise— still—gave cause for small complaints. "Enough power is at hand; one can reach 100 kph in 7.2 seconds", John Lamm wrote in 1983. "But the Corvette offers more than mere speed. For example, fully new seat comfort. Now one no longer has the feeling of sitting in a huge shoe that is still too narrow . . ." There was a good panoramic view, a wealth of instrumentation (optionally changed to metric indications, which was very welcome) and, happily, no superfulous nonsense. "Is the Corvette the best exotic car in the world?" It was compared with a Porsche 928 S and a Ferrari 308 GTBi, and the conclusion was drawn that the American car didn't

come off so badly at all . . . In particular, the car was superior to its European rivals in design (said author Jonathan Thompson): "It is the best-looking car on the market today . . . not only exciting but also tasteful and elegant . . . With this Corvette, the spotlight of body design have turned from Europe to America . . ." A compliment that was meant for Jerry Palmer, the "Corvette Body Designer" who was also responsible for the Camaro and the Chevrolet Vega.

Dream car of the Nineties: the Chevrolet Corvette displayed at Geneva in 1989, with 5.7 liter motor, four valves and all the attributes of modern high-performance motor construction.

Model year	Motor specifications		Fuel system	Notes
1953	6-Cylinder Blue Flame		3 Side-draft carburetors	300 pre-series cars, all white
1954	235 c. i. (3858 cc)	150 HP/4200 ohv	3 Side-draft carburetors	Colors now also red, blue, copper
1955	Blue Flame 235 c. i. (3858 cc) Turbo Fire V-8 265 c. i. (4343 cc)	155 HP/4200 ohv 195 HP/4400 ohv	3 Side-draft carburetors 1 4-throat downdraft carburetor	New: V-8 motor, 12 volt system; Some cars with 3-speed manual transmission
1956	V-8 265 c. i. (4343 cc)	210 HP/5200 ohv 225 HP/5200 ohv	1 4-throat downdraft carburetor 2 4-throat downdraft carburetors	New body; 3-speed transmission; Powerglide optional
1957	V-8 283 c. i. (4638 cc) Competition	220 HP/4800 ohv 245 HP/5000 ohv 250 HP/5000 ohv 283 HP/ 6200 ohv	1 4-throat downdraft carburetor 2 4-throat downdraft carburetors Ramjet Fuel Injection Ramjet Fuel Injection	Optional 4-speed transmission
1958	V-8 283 c. i. (4638 cc) Competition	230HP/4800 ohv 245 HP/5000 ohv 250 HP/5000 ohv 290 HP/6200 ohv	1 4-throat downdraft carburetor 2 4-throat downdraft carburetors Ramjet Fuel Injection Ramjet Fuel Injection	New grille and dual headlights, more chrome
1959	V-8 283 c. i. (4638 cc)	230 HP/4800 ohv 245 HP/5000 ohv 250 HP/5000 ohv 270 HP/5400 ohv 290 HP/6200 ohv	1 4-throat downdraft carburetor 2 4-throat downdraft carburetors Ramjet Fuel Injection 2 4-throat downdraft carburetors Ramjet Fuel Injection	Chrome is reduced again
1960	V-8 283 c. i. (4638 cc)	230 HP/4800 ohv 245 HP/5000 ohv 270 HP/5400 ohv 275 HP/5800 ohv 315 HP/6400 ohv	1 4-throat downdraft carburetor 2 4-throat downdraft carburetors 2 4-throat downdraft carburetors Ramjet Fuel Injection Ramjet Fuel Injection	Electric windows optional
1961	V-8 283 c. i. (4638 cc)	as 1960	as 1960	New grille, new tail
1962	V-8 327 c. i. (5359 cc)	250 HP/4400 ohv 300 HP/5000 ohv 340 HP/6000 ohv 360 HP/6000 ohv	1 4-throat downdraft carburetor 1 4-throat downdraft carburetor 1 4-throat downdraft carburetor Ranjet Fuel Injection	New "327" motor

Technical Data

Model year	Motor specifications		Fuel system	Notes
1963	V-8 327 c. i. (5359 cc)	as 1962	as 1962	New body, new fastback coupe
1964	V-8 327 c. i. (5359 cc)	250 HP/4400 ohv	1 4-throat downdraft carburetor	Adjustable shock absorbers
		300 HP/5000 ohv	1 4-throat downdraft carburetor	
		365 HP/6200 ohv	1 4-throat downdraft carburetor	
		375 HP/6200 ohv	Fuel injection	
1965	V-8 327 c. i. (5359 cc)	250 HP/4400 ohv	1 4-throat downdraft carburetor	Four disc brakes
		300 HP/5000 ohv	1 4-throat downdraft carburetor	
		350 HP/5800 ohv	1 4-throat downdraft carburetor	
		365 HP/6200 ohv	1 4-throat downdraft carburetor	
		375 HP/6200 ohv	Fuel injection	
	V-8 396 c. i. (6489 cc)	HP/4800 ohv	2 4-throat downdraft carburetors	
1966	V-8 327 c. i. (5359 cc)	300 HP/5000 ohv	1 4-throat downdraft carburetor	New Turbo Jet 427 c. i. motor
		350 HP/5800 ohv	1 4-throat downdraft carburetor	
	Turbo Jet 427 c. i. (6997 cc)	390 HP/5200 ohv	1 4-throat downdraft carburetor	
	V-8	425 HP/5600 ohv	1 4-throat downdraft carburetor	
1967	V-8 327 c. i. (5359 cc)	300 HP/5000 ohv	1 4-throat downdraft carburetor	New double-carb high-performance motors
		350 HP/5800 ohv	1 4-throat downdraft carburetor	
	Turbo Jet 427 c. i. (6997 cc)	390 HP/5400 ohv	1 4-throat downdraft carburetor	
	V-8	400 HP/5400 ohv	3 double carburetors	
		435 HP/5800 ohv	3 double carburetors	
1968	V-8 327 c. i. (5359 cc)	300 HP/5000 ohv	1 4-throat downdraft carburetor	New body styling
	V-8 396 c. i. (6489 cc)	350 HP/5200 ohv	1 4-throat downdraft carburetor	
	V-8 427 c. i. (6997 cc)	390 HP/5400 ohv	1 4-throat downdraft carburetor	
		400 HP/5400 ohv	3 double carburetors	
		435 HP/5800 ohv	3 double carburetors	
1969	V-8 427 c. i. (5735 cc)	300 HP/4800 ohv	1 4-throat downdraft carburetor	New 350 c. i. motor
		350 HP/5600 ohv	1 4-throat downdraft carburetor	
	V-8 427 c. i. (6997 cc)	390 HP/5400 ohv	1 4-throat downdraft carburetor	
		400 HP/5400 ohv	1 4-throat downdraft carburetor	
		425 HP/5600 ohv	1 4-throat downdraft carburetor	
		430 HP/5200 ohv	1 4-throat downdraft carburetor	
		435 HP/5800 ohv	3 double carburetors	

Technical Data

Model year	Motor specifications		Fuel system	Notes
1970	V-8 350 c. i. (5735 cc)	300 HP/4800 ohv	1 4-throat downdraft carburetor	New 454 c. i. motor
		350 HP/5600 ohv	1 4-throat downdraft carburetor	
		370 HP/6000 ohv	1 4-throat downdraft carburetor	
	V-8 454 c. i. (7440 cc)	390 HP/4800 ohv	1 4-throat downdraft carburetor	
		460 HP/5600 ohv	1 4-throat downdraft carburetor	
1971	V-8 350 c. i. (5735 cc)	270 HP/4800 ohv	1 4-throat downdraft carburetor	
		330 HP/5600 ohv	1 4-throat downdraft carburetor	
	V-8 454 c. i. (7440 cc)	365 HP/4800 ohv	1 4-throat downdraft carburetor	
		425 HP/5600 ohv	1 4-throat downdraft carburetor	
1972	V-8 350 c. i. (5735 cc)	200 HP/4400 ohv	1 4-throat downdraft carburetor	Drastic lowering of performance
		255 HP/5600 ohv	1 4-throat downdraft carburetor	
	V-8 454 c. i. (7440 cc)	270 HP/4000 ohv	1 4-throat downdraft carburetor	
1973	V-8 350 c. i. (5735 cc)	190 HP/4400 ohv	1 4-throat downdraft carburetor	
		250 HP/5200 ohv	1 4-throat downdraft carburetor	
	V-8 454 c. i. (7440 cc)	275 HP/4000 ohv	1 4-throat downdraft carburetor	
1974	V-8 350 c. i. (5735 cc)	195 HP/4400 ohv	1 4-throat downdraft carburetor	New collision-safe rear
		250 HP/5200 ohv	1 4-throat downdraft carburetor	
	V-8 454 c. i. (7440 cc)	270 HP/4400 ohv	1 4-throat downdraft carburetor	
1975	V-8 350 c. i. (5735 cc)	198 HP/4400 ohv	1 4-throat downdraft carburetor	
		253 HP/5200 ohv	1 4-throat downdraft carburetor	
	V-8 454 c. i. (7440 cc)	247 HP/4400 ohv	1 4-throat downdraft carburetor	
1976	V-8 350 c. i. (5735 cc)	167 HP/3800 ohv	1 4-throat downdraft carburetor	
		208 HP/4800 ohv	1 4-throat downdraft carburetor	
1977	V-8 350 c. i. (5735 cc)	183 HP/4000 ohv	1 4-throat downdraft carburetor	
		213 HP/5200 ohv	1 4-throat downdraft carburetor	
1978	V-8 350 c. i. (5735 cc)	180 HP/4000 ohv	1 4-throat downdraft carburetor	Standard disc brakes
		210 HP/5200 ohv	1 4-throat downdraft carburetor	
1979	V-8 350 c. i. (5735 cc)	185 HP/4000 ohv	1 4-throat downdraft carburetor	Independent rear suspension
		220 HP/5200 ohv	1 4-throat downdraft carburetor	

Technical Data

Model year	Motor specifications		Fuel system	Notes
1980	V-8 350 c. i. (5735 cc)	195 HP/4000 ohv 225 HP/5200 ohv	1 4-throat downdraft carburetor 1 4-throat downdraft carburetor	Weight reduced by 140 kg
1981	V-8 305 c. i. (5001 cc) V-8 350 c. i. (5735 cc)	186 HP/4200 ohv 197 HP/4400 ohv 238 HP/5200 ohv	1 4-throat downdraft carburetor 1 4-throat downdraft carburetor 1 4-throat downdraft carburetor	
1982	V-8 350 c. i. (5735 cc)	197 HP/4400 ohv	1 4-throat downdraft carburetor	Collector edition; opening rear trunk
1983	V-8 350 c. i. (5735 cc)	204 HP/4200 ohv	Fuel injection	Completely new model
1984-85	V-8 350 c. i. (5735 cc)	208 HP/4200 ohv	Fuel injection	
1986	V-8 350 c. i. (5735 cc)	208 HP/4200 ohv	Fuel injection	New convertible

Technical Data